Buses
in camera
SCOTLAND

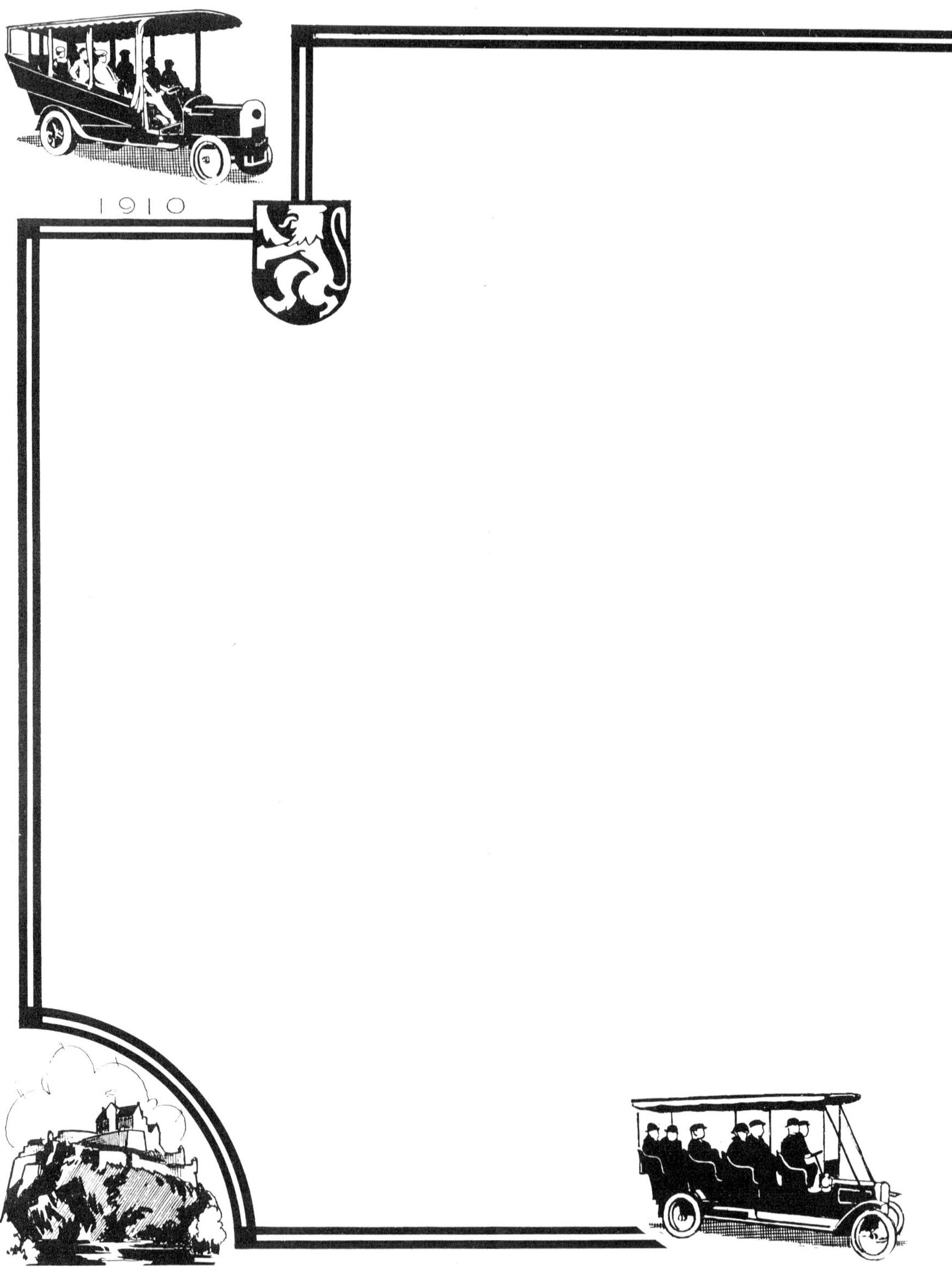
1910

Buses in camera
SCOTLAND

GAVIN BOOTH

LONDON
IAN ALLAN LTD

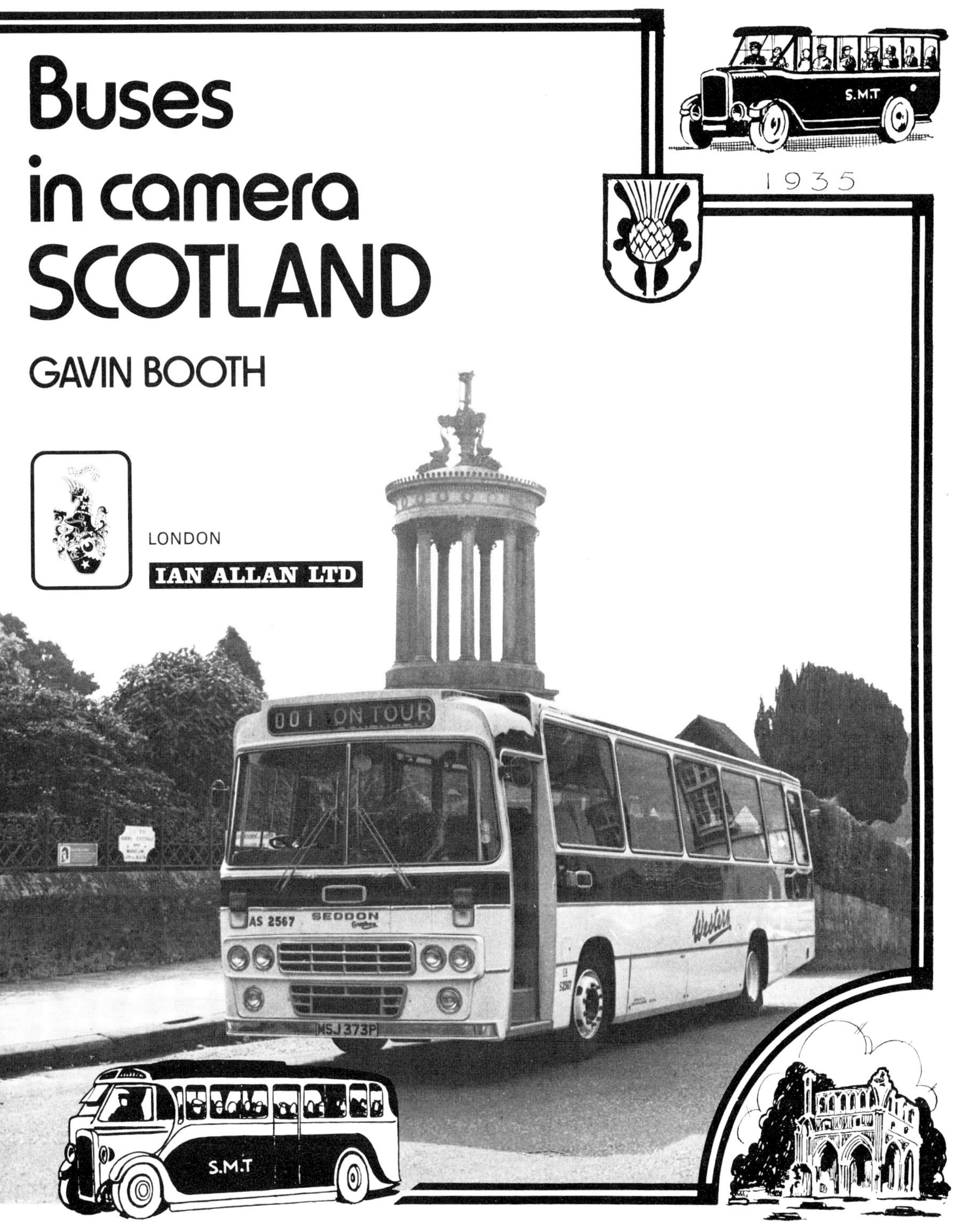

First published 1978

ISBN 0 7110 0879 5

Published by Ian Allan Ltd, Shepperton, Surrey,
and Printed in the United Kingdom by
Ian Allan Printing Ltd.

Contents

Introduction

The discovery of North Sea oil, and the prospect of a Scottish Assembly have meant that interest in Scotland has been intense in the last few years. Scotland's importance to the economic and social development of the United Kingdom has, it seems, been acknowledged at last.

Things have also been happening in the structure of Scotland's transport network, with the formation of the Greater Glasgow PTE in 1973, and the changes which followed local government reorganisation in 1975, so *Buses in Camera: Scotland* comes at an opportune time. Scotland was originally covered in *Buses in Camera: Scotland and Northern England*, published in 1973, but this new edition is devoted solely to Scotland and includes, for the first time, a number of photographs portraying the tramcars which played such an important part in the life of Scotland's four main cities until the 1950s and 1960s.

As before, 1930 and the birth of the 'modern' bus is taken as a convenient starting point, and the book covers the bus and tram scene in Scotland since that time, with special regard to the many interesting developments in the few years since the appearance of the original book.

The photographs which I have included were chosen to record some of the many interesting buses and trams which have worked in Scotland over the last 50 years, and to portray them in their natural surroundings, from the desolation of the Outer Hebrides to the congestion of central Glasgow.

I have split the book into three main sections, dealing with the Scottish Bus Group, the Local Authority fleets, and the Independents; in addition there are photo-features on specific subjects.

The Scots have always tended to support local industry, and many of the buses bought for use in Scotland have been partly or wholly built north of the Border. In this book you will find examples of these — chassis and underframes built by Albion at Scotstoun and Ailsa at Irvine, and bodies built by Alexander, Cowieson, Croft, Pickering, Scottish Aviation and Walker.

Scotland still retains much of the transport variety which seems to be disappearing from other areas. The Scottish Bus Group fleets still contain an interesting variety of vehicle types, and the four local authority fleets pursue individual buying policies; the surviving independents add to the interest in certain areas, and soldier on resolutely; and there is the Post Office, a growing force in the rural transport scene, with its fast-expanding network of Postbus services.

In short, there is a lot to see in Scotland, and I have endeavoured to capture some of this variety in the book.

Edinburgh, 1978   *Gavin Booth*

A line of football special cars awaits the crowds from Aberdeen's Pittodrie Park in 1939. The front car, 74, was one of six cars built for Aberdeen Corporation in 1913 by J. T. Clark, a local bodybuilder.

Scottish Bus Group

The Scottish Bus Group story really started in Edinburgh in 1905 when a number of ambitious businessmen registered the Scottish Motor Traction Company Limited. SMT could easily have become just another of the over-ambitious schemes to capitalise on the motor bus, which was still very much in its infancy at the time. Even the name — the *Scottish* Motor Traction Company — was ambitious for a firm whose horizons were initially strictly limited to the Edinburgh and West Lothian areas.

But SMT had one special ingredient, a shrewd young engineer called William Thomson, and from its first day of operation, 1 January 1906, the company was an instant success, and its services and tours spread rapidly outwards from Edinburgh. Much of the growth in the 1920s was through take-overs of the many other firms which had sprung up at the time, but which had lacked the sound business acumen of those in control of SMT.

The year 1928 marked the end of the first chapter in the SMT story, for as the bus industry had grown and the buses improved, the main-line railway companies were suffering from the competition. They campaigned against this and were rewarded in 1928 with powers to operate bus services. Wisely they chose mainly to buy into existing bus companies, in preference to competing directly. In Scotland, LMS and LNER bought into SMT and a new Scottish Motor Traction company was formed in 1929. The new SMT was more than simply a local operator; it became the holding company for two growing bus companies with railway shareholdings, W. Alexander & Sons of Falkirk, and Midland Bus Services of Airdrie.

The Alexander family had started running buses in 1919, mainly in the area between Falkirk and Glasgow and by 1928 had extended north as far as Perth and Dundee. Midland was based on Airdrie and operated mainly in Lanarkshire and into Ayrshire.

SMT and Alexanders, as the main constituents, immediately set about consolidating their position with a long series of take-overs. SMT already had a firm foothold in the Lothians and the Borders and had extended its territory to reach Newcastle in 1928 and Lancashire in 1930, on services joint with United and Ribble. The take-over of a smaller Edinburgh firm brought a London service and SMT started operating a daily service between Edinburgh and London in April 1930. Alexanders, on the other hand, was expanding in Scotland. Take-overs in the decade from 1929 gave Alexanders a useful network in Fife and in the north-east of Scotland and Alexanders buses eventually replaced tramways in Kirkcaldy, Falkirk

and Dunfermline and municipally-owned buses in Perth.

The LMS and LNER each had about 25% of SMT's shares and were anxious to see that most of their bus-operating interests in Scotland were exercised through SMT. This created problems in the west of Scotland, where the BET-owned Scottish General Transport company, based on Kilmarnock, was an important operator. The problem of ownership was solved when BET sold Scottish Transport to SMT in 1931. Now SMT had two large fleets operating in similar areas — mainly to the south-west of Glasgow; there was Midland, in SMT control since 1929, and now Scottish Transport. The obvious solution was a merger of the fleets and Scottish Transport became Western SMT in 1932, SMT's subsidiary in Renfrewshire, Ayrshire and the south-west. Other SMT acquisitions passed into Western control, as did some local services started by the LMS Railway. Western buses replaced municipal trams at Ayr and municipal buses at Kilmarnock in 1932.

In the Lanarkshire area, to the south of Glasgow and, to a lesser degree on the north bank of the Clyde in Dunbartonshire, there was the Glasgow General Omnibus & Motor Services, better known as GOC. There were close associations between GOC and LGOC — London General — in its early days and, from its formation in 1926, GOC operated a very un-Scottish fleet of AEC and ADC models, including some London-style double-deckers. LMS baled GOC out in 1930 when it got into financial difficulties and the same year LMS bought over two important Lanarkshire operators, Stewart & McDonald of Carluke, and Torrance of Hamilton. In 1932 Stewart & McDonald and Torrance were absorbed by GOC and later that year GOC was renamed Central SMT.

So now there were the four main SMT companies, covering between them most of south and central Scotland, and up into the north-east.

The strains of World War 2 left SMT with a time-worn fleet of buses in 1945 and it was clearly going to be a costly exercise if they were to aspire to the standard of service offered in 1939. The postwar travel boom created extra problems and voluntary nationalisation in 1949 was seen as the solution which was most in the public interest.

So the SMT bus interests passed into the control of the British Transport Commission and the private car business retained the familiar 'SMT' name, while the Edinburgh-based SMT bus company became Scottish Omnibuses Ltd. A fifth company joined what was to become known as the Scottish Bus Group in 1951, when Highland Omnibuses was formed, based on Inverness. The BTC had inherited the former LMS shareholding in The Highland Transport Company in 1948, and in 1951 management was passed to Scottish Omnibuses. BTC had also acquired Macrae & Dick in 1951, so these services passed to Highland, as did the Alexanders services based on Inverness.

The Scottish Group faced the familiar problems of the 1950s, and continued to operate successfully under London-based holding companies, returning an annual profit. The number of SBG subsidiaries increased to seven in 1961 when the giant Alexanders empire was split into three more manageable units, Alexanders (Midland), based on Falkirk, Alexanders (Fife) based on Kirkcaldy, and Alexanders (Northern), based on Aberdeen.

Control of SBG returned to Scotland when the Scottish Transport Group was formed in 1969. From its Edinburgh headquarters STG encompassed the buses of SBG and the ships of the Caledonian Steam Packet Company and David MacBrayne. The MacBrayne interests also included a sizeable bus fleet operating in the West Highlands and on many of the islands, but the MacBrayne buses soon passed into the control of Highland Omnibuses and, in the case of the Glasgow-Campbeltown service, Western SMT.

Right: A reminder of 'the SMT', still to be seen in 1978 in the yard of the Scottish independent Hutchison, Overtown. It is an Albion Valkyrie with a Cowieson body, new to SMT in 1931 as A98. It survived only eight years before withdrawal and sale to Jackson, Auchenheath, and although its future is uncertain, it would be a pity if this all-Scottish vehicle was allowed to rot away. *Below:* A newer Cowieson body was fitted to this SMT Leyland Tiger TS7, one of ten 34-seat buses supplied in 1935. Eight of its brothers were rebodied as double-deckers during World War 2, but H110 survived in this state until 1955. It is seen late in its life in Queen Street, Edinburgh.

Left: Detail from an appealingly naive SMT coach tour advertisement in 1936. *Below:* The 1937 family taking an SMT tour might well have travelled on a fine Leyland Tiger TS7 like this Duple-bodied 30-seater, one of eight delivered that year. Although Duple bodies were favoured for SMT's smaller Bedford coaches, these were the only full-size Duple bodies bought at the time. This coach, H202, was withdrawn in 1954.

SMT's last normal peacetime-style deliveries, in 1940, were Alexander-bodied AEC Regals and Leyland Tigers with short bonnets and cabs to allow a seating capacity of 39. This Regal, one of 20, passed in 1961 to the Musselburgh contractor Crudens, in whose yellow livery it is seen here.

SMT received only three 'unfrozen' buses
in 1942, and two were AEC Regents with
Brush 55-seat bodies, the first of many
AEC double-deckers in the fleet. BB1 is
seen at St Andrew Square, Edinburgh, in
the pre-1949 blue livery; it was
withdrawn in 1955.

Other wartime deliveries included six of
these Strachan-bodied utility Dennis
Lancet IIs. S6 is seen in Dalry Road,
Edinburgh, in 1953, the year before it
was withdrawn and sold to Stark,
Dunbar.

After the War, SMT was quick to re-start
its important touring programme, and did
so with coaches like the 32 Bedford OBs
supplied in 1947/48 with SMT bodies to
the Duple Vista design.

Facing page: SOL received 40 AEC
Regent IIIs in 1950, 20 with Duple
bodies, and 20, like BB97 shown here,
had stylish Burlingham bodies. It is
shown at the company's main depot at
New Street, Edinburgh.

08D
EDINBURGH VIA LITTLE FRANCE
BB97
Regent

The next double-deckers bought by SOL were the 15 Bristol Lodekka LD6Gs delivered in 1956, with Eastern Coach Works 60-seat bodies. As part of BTC, the Scottish Group companies could buy Bristol/ECW products as well as buses available on the open market. AA4 is seen in St Andrew Square, Edinburgh, when new. *Right:* When SOL acquired Lowland Motorways, the Glasgow independent in 1958, it took over a mixed fleet of vehicles. Among the more recent buses were two all-Leyland Titan PD2/12s, bought new in 1954. HH6 is seen at Cunningham Street, Glasgow in 1965, still in SOL's light green livery, with 'Scottish' fleetname. *Below right:* Sister vehicle HH7 leaving St Andrew Square bus station wearing the darker Lothian Green livery and Eastern Scottish fleetname adopted in 1964.

Far right: A Baxter-ordered bus delivered new to SOL in 1963 was an AEC/Park Royal Bridgemaster, which became BB962. It is seen on North Bridge, Edinburgh, with BB18 at the rear, another Bridgemaster which had been delivered to Baxter in 1961, as seen in the inset view. A third Bridgemaster, also ordered by Baxter, was exchanged for an AEC Renown.

12

Another notable SOL take-over was the acquisition of the famous independent Baxter of Airdrie in 1962. Baxter vehicles are covered on page 16, but SOL also inherited vehicles ordered by Baxter, and delivered new after the take-over. These included DD961, a Daimler Fleetline with low-height 73-seat Alexander body, seen here leaving Buchanan Street bus station in Glasgow when new in 1963. It was the Bus Group's first Fleetline, and had the first Alexander D type body — though this was burnt out in 1965, and it received a similar 74-seat body in 1966, by which time it had actually joined the subsidiary Baxter fleet, which retained the familiar blue livery and fleetname as a local goodwill gesture.

Standard SOL single-deck deliveries from 1960 to 1962 were 30ft AEC Reliances with 41-seat Alexander dual-purpose bodies. B830, a 1961 example, is seen in the Border town of Melrose in 1963.

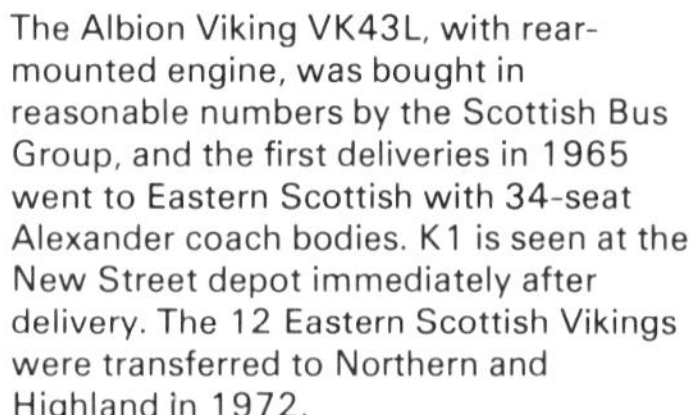

The Albion Viking VK43L, with rear-mounted engine, was bought in reasonable numbers by the Scottish Bus Group, and the first deliveries in 1965 went to Eastern Scottish with 34-seat Alexander coach bodies. K1 is seen at the New Street depot immediately after delivery. The 12 Eastern Scottish Vikings were transferred to Northern and Highland in 1972.

Following problems with early examples of the rear-engined Bristol VRT double-decker, the SBG exchanged its VRTs in 1973 for National Bus Company Lodekkas. The first NBC Lodekka to reach Eastern Scottish was United Counties 736, but when it was discovered that it was an FLF6*B* model, with Bristol engine, it returned to England to be replaced by Gardner-engined examples from various sources. The United Counties bus is shown leaving New Street depot in Edinburgh.

The Alexander Y type body first appeared in SBG fleets in 1963, although the prototypes were built in 1961. Literally thousands have been built for the Group since that time, on a variety of chassis types, and in bus, dual-purpose and coach format. Eastern Scottish received Y types on AEC Reliance, Albion Viking, Bedford VAM, YRQ and YRT, Bristol LH and RE, Leyland Leopard and Seddon Pennine chassis. This 49-seat dual-purpose Leopard is seen at Nottingham in 1975 on the Edinburgh-Leicester service.

Probably the most famous of the Scottish
independents was the smart fleet of
Baxter of Airdrie. When Scottish
Omnibuses took over in 1962, the Baxter
blue livery was dropped, but was
restored after local objections, and was
worn by SOL vehicles at Airdrie's Victoria
depot until 1977. This Leyland Tiger Cub
with Burlingham body was new in 1954,
but had been withdrawn before the take-
over.

Right: Baxter buses brought a welcome
splash of colour to the grey streets of
Airdrie and Coatbridge, uncompromising
industrial towns. Some of the
atmosphere is conveyed in this view at
Coatbridge Fountain, with Baxter 107, an
all-Leyland Royal Tiger PSU1/17
44-seater. It was new in 1952 and
passed to SOL in 1962.

An older Baxter Leyland, a 1931 TD1
Titan with Cowieson body, which started
life with Glasgow Corporation and passed
to Baxter via Graham of Paisley.

Right: The last four Titans delivered to
Baxter had unusual lowbridge forward-
entrance Massey 56-seat bodies. The
first was 74, new in 1960.

Stark of Dunbar was an independent which had an unusual relationship with the Scottish Group. Part of the business was acquired by SMT in 1928 along with a share in the Dunbar-Edinburgh service; Stark buses on this route carried SMT and ultimately SOL fleetnames. The remainder of the fleet wore the Stark name, like this 1951 Leyland Royal Tiger PSU1/15 with 39-seat Burlingham body.

The Stark business was fully absorbed by Scottish Omnibuses in 1964, and the light green livery and Stark fleetnames were retained, and eventually applied to vehicles transferred from the parent SOL fleet. At Dunbar depot in 1965 was B673, a 1959 AEC Reliance/Alexander 38-seat coach transferred to Stark in 1964, and C22, a 'genuine' Stark vehicle, a Bedford OB/Duple 29-seater, now preserved.

OPERATE
TO AND FROM ALL
THE PRINCIPAL CENTRES IN
THE NORTH OF SCOTLAND

GLASGOW TO

Aberdeen   Dundee   Perth
Montrose   Stonehaven   Oban
Inverness   Crieff   Callander
Stirling   Dunfermline   Alloa
Kirkcaldy   Leven   St. Andrews
etc., etc., etc.

There are Connecting Services at all
these points to all the neighbouring
towns.

There are 28 Alexander Depots all
over Scotland, including :

Aberdeen (2), Arbroath, Braemar,
Ballater, Buckie, Cupar, Crieff,
Dundee, Dunfermline, Elgin,
Forfar, Montrose, Stirling, and
Stonehaven.

For Speed, Comfort and Safety
GO BY ALEXANDER'S

EDINBURGH TO ABERDEEN

Leaves CHAMBERS ST. at 9.30 a.m.
Arrives ABERDEEN ... 4.30 p.m.
(*Via* Falkirk, Dundee and Montrose)

24/- LIMITED **12/-**
RETURN STOP SINGLE

The joys of coach travel in the 1930s,
Alexanders style.

Top: Albions were plentiful in the
Alexanders fleet in the early 1930s. This
was D65, an Albion PJ24, new as a
normal control vehicle to Armstrong &
Siddle, Keswick, in 1927. It passed to
Ribble and then to Alexanders, who sent

it to Forbes Brebner of Crieff for the
forward control body shown. It is in the
livery of Pender of Falkirk, an Alexander
subsidiary; W. Alexander & Sons are
shown on the legal lettering as
'Proprietors'.

From the 1930s to the 1950s, Leyland
double-deckers dominated the
Alexanders fleet, and this was an early
example. R35, an all-Leyland Titan TD2,
was one of 12 delivered in 1932, and
was withdrawn in 1950. It worked in the
Northern Area, and is seen being washed
at Aberdeen.

Above: Another odd Albion was E19, a Northern Counties-bodied Venturer M81 built in 1933 as an Albion demonstrator. Although in Alexanders livery, it was still a demonstrator when photographed here; it was bought in 1933, and lasted until 1955.

At one time the Alexanders fleet had an interesting selection of older vehicles retained for use as tow wagons. The Perth tow wagon in the early 1950s was based on an ex-Scottish General 1929 Lion LT1, seen here at Perth Station alongside a 1939 Leyland Tiger TS8 with Alexander 35-seat body transferred from SMT with the Dundee area services in 1950.

A Cheetah strays from its home territory. K27 was one of the large fleet of Leyland's lightweight Cheetah LZ2A model taken into Alexanders ownership in 1938. The 35-seat body was built by Burlingham, and it is seen here boarding the steam ferry *Tessa* at Tilbury en route for Eire on a Harland Engineering official tour of England and Eire in 1946.

The immaculate and long-lived vehicles of the Alexanders fleet were well-known in the 1950s and 1960s. It was possible to see vehicles like this on normal service until 1963, by which time they actually belonged to the fleet of Alexanders (Midland), following the three-way split of the giant Alexanders empire in 1961. Laying-over at Falkirk in 1963 were R321, a 1941 all-Leyland Titan TD7 and RO471, a 1944 Daimler CWA6 with Brush body.

Another long-lived bus in the Alexanders fleet was P416, a 1937 Leyland Tiger TS7 with an Alexander 32-seat bus body. It is seen here in town service red livery on a Kirkcaldy town service in 1960, before the formation of Alexanders (Fife). P416 survived to pass into the Fife fleet.

RO570 was actually new to Greig, Inverness in 1945, a Guy Arab II with Northern Counties 56-seat body, and passed to Alexanders in 1947. It is seen in town red livery at Kirkcaldy town bus station in 1963; it survived until 1966.

Many of these utility SMT-bodied
Bedford OWBs entered the Alexanders
fleet during World War 2. W159 was
new in 1945, and is seen in the early
1950s at Macduff depot, in the Northern
Area.

When it was photographed at Pitlochry in
1960, PA66 was the only one-man bus
in the Alexanders fleet. It was a 1948
Leyland Tiger PS1 with Alexander
35-seat body.

After its large deliveries of Leyland Tiger PS1s in 1947-50, Alexanders followed with a batch of 20 of the larger-engined OPS2/1 Tigers in 1951. These had Alexander 35-seat bodies, and PB13 is seen at Minehead on the Devon and Cornwall extended tour in 1958. Most of the PB class were converted to PS1 standard in 1960, and 'new' double-deckers appeared in 1961 using the 0600 engines and other units from these vehicles.

The Nimbus was one of the later Albion models which passed through the Alexanders fleet. This 1960 NS3L Nimbus with 29-seat Alexander body is seen on the Dukes Road, in the Trossachs, during the Omnibus Society Presidential Weekend in 1961.

W. Alexander & Sons Ltd was split into
three separate companies in 1961, and
Alexanders (Fife), based on Kirkcaldy,
took over the former Fife Area. FPA26, a
1947 Leyland Tiger PS1 with Alexander
body, is seen in Fife red livery in 1965,
pressed into service on the long route to
St Andrews on the first Saturday of the
annual Glasgow Fair holiday.

Its link with the British Transport
Commission brought many Bristol
vehicles into SBG fleets. Most were
Lodekkas, but there were also LSs, MWs
and REs, and, more recently, LHs and
VRTs. The only ECW *bus* bodied LSs for
the Group were 20 LS6Gs supplied to
Alexanders in 1955, and which worked
from the Fife Area all their lives. FE9 is
seen in Perth.

The first production batch of the Scottish-built front-engined Volvo Ailsa model were 40 vehicles supplied to Alexanders (Fife) in 1975. FRA10, with Alexander 79-seat body, is seen at Crossgates on the busy 314 service from Dunfermline.

Duple-bodied Fords were delivered to all three of the Alexanders companies in the 1970s, like Fife FT1, a 45-seat Dominant body on R1014 chassis, seen here in the historic town of Falkland.

Among the elderly vehicles which survived into the Falkirk-based Alexanders (Midland) fleet was P684, one of two rare 'unfrozen' Leyland Tiger TS11s with 34-seat Willowbrook bodies, delivered in 1942. It is seen here at Dundas Street bus station, Glasgow, in 1964, the year it was withdrawn. It is now preserved.

Another unusual veteran to wear Midland blue was RO451, a Guy Arab II, new in 1943 with Roe body. It received this ECW body in 1951, and lasted until 1965, when it became an open-top tree-lopper.

MRA34, a 1948 Leyland Titan PD1 with
Alexander 53-seat body, photographed
near Gartcosh in 1967, late in its life.

The last of a long line of side gangway
lowbridge Leyland Titans supplied to
Alexanders were PD3A/3 models
delivered in 1961 to the Midland and
Northern fleets. MRB266, one of the
Midland vehicles, is seen in Glasgow in
1963 in a short-lived experimental livery
variation.

The three Alexanders fleets were the largest SBG users of the rear-engined Albion Viking VK43L model. This is MNV23 of 1967, with the inevitable Alexander Y type body, in the Kildrum area of the new town of Cumbernauld.

Successors to the lowbridge Leyland Titans in several SBG fleets were low-height Albion Lowlanders. Two Alexander-bodied Midland Lowlanders are seen one evening in 1963 at Drumchapel terminus, in suburban Glasgow.

From 1958 to 1961, most single-deck
deliveries to the Alexanders fleet carried
this style of Alexander dual-purpose
body. MAC177, a 1960 AEC Reliance
41-seater, is seen in 1967 leaving
Allandale.

The 1962 single-deckers for the freshly-
split Alexanders companies had this
unusual style of Alexander body, based
on the design supplied to BET fleets, but
with an SBG-style front end. MPD229, a
Leyland Tiger Cub PSUC1/2 41-seater, is
seen at Oban in 1968, when there was a
Midland depot in the town. In 1970 the
isolated Oban operation was transferred
to Highland ownership. This bus was
actually transferred to Highland with the
Oban services, but returned to Midland,
in exchange for an AEC Reliance.

The statue of William Wallace in Aberdeen indicates the way for NRE1, one of two Albion Lowlander LR1s with 71-seat Alexander bodies supplied to Alexanders (Northern) in 1961. The Aberdeen-based Northern company wears a yellow livery.

Although the Bedford VAS1 model was familiar in the Alexanders fleets with Duple Bella Vista coach body, the three companies received only a handful of these VAS1s with Duple Midland 30-seat bus bodies. NW264 was Northern's first example, seen in 1966 outside the depot of the former independent operator, Strachan of Ballater.

An unusual disposal for a Northern bus — NRA96 photographed in 1973 at the Essex premises of Omnibus Promotions, a firm specialising in exporting mock London Transport buses. Lowbridge exposed-radiator buses were preferred, and this 1948 Leyland Titan PD1A with Leyland body is here in full London Transport livery, complete with fleetnames. It was new to Sutherland, Peterhead, and passed to Alexanders in 1950.

Above: Between 1969 and 1973, Scottish Omnibuses transferred 26 of its 11metre AEC Reliance 590s with Alexander 49-seat bodies to the Highland and Northern fleets. Northern NAC261, new in 1966, is seen early in 1970 in snow-covered Aberdeen.

Below: Northern has built up a large Ford fleet in recent years, and NT145, a 1976 R1114 with Duple Dominant body, is seen leaving Dundee, bound for Aberdeen.

A period scene in Main Street,
Rutherglen in 1936, with a Chevrolet
truck, Glasgow Corporation standard
tram 483, a Rolls-Royce car and Central
SMT L4, a Leyland Titan TD1 with
51-seat lowbridge Leyland body. It was
new in 1929 to Glasgow General, the
firm which in 1932 became Central SMT.

A later Central Titan, L96, a 1937 TD4
with smart 53-seat Leyland body. It
survived until 1958.

Although in prewar days Central SMT acquired many Albions from firms which passed into its control, new Albions only figured in the 1932 vehicle orders. These included 40 of the new Valiant PV70 model, with 32-seat rear-entrance bodies by Pickering and Metro-Cammell. Pickering-bodied examples figured in this contemporary advertisement (*below*) and official photo.

THE NEW ALBION
"VALIANT"
SINGLE DECKER

Albion

ALBION MOTORS LTD.
SCOTSTOUN, GLASGOW, W.4.
London: - - BANK BUILDINGS
20 KINGSWAY, W.C.2.

Also at MANCHESTER, LEEDS,
SHEFFIELD, BIRMINGHAM, BRISTOL
and EDINBURGH.

Guys were favoured in the Central fleet for several years, in addition to the traditional Leylands. H47 was one of 16 Guy Arab IIIs supplied in 1951 with an unusual style of lowbridge Guy body. It was photographed at Wishaw depot in 1961.

There were single-deck Guys too, like K26, a 1952 Arab III with 37-seat Guy rear-entrance body.

In 1954 Central received ten of these Guy Arab UFs with rare 43-seat rear-entrance Alexander Coronation-style bodies; these were SBG's last rear-entrance single-deckers and the last Coronation bodies built. K45 is seen in 1965 at Lanark bus station.

In direct line from L96 on page 32, L468 was a 1953 Titan PD2/1 with 53-seat Leyland body, which lasted until 1968.

The very last of Central's long line of Leyland Titans, L631, a PD2/30 model with 59-seat body, is collected from Alexander's Falkirk coachworks in 1960. It lasted until 1975.

Various models of Bristol Lodekka were
delivered to Central SMT between 1955
and 1967. These included the only FSF
(short, forward-entrance) models
supplied to an SBG fleet, like B159 on
the right of this pair parked in Glasgow
during the construction of Buchanan bus
station. B185 is a 1964 FS6G model.

One of the two prototype Bristol VRLs
built in 1966 was loaned to Central SMT
from 1966 to 1970. It had a
longtitudinally-mounted Gardner engine,
and though it was followed by a 1969
order for the more conventional VRT
model, these did not last long and were
exchanged with NBC for Lodekkas in
1973.

Highland Omnibuses, formed in 1952 as
the Inverness-based SBG subsidiary, was
built on the businesses of local
operators, together with services
developed by Alexanders. With the
Alexanders services came 20 Leyland
double-deckers, mostly fairly elderly
machines, including 12 Leyland
Tiger TS7s converted to Titan TD4
standard and rebodied during World
War 2. J150 was new in 1935 as
Alexanders P253, and received this
Alexander lowbridge body in 1943,
becoming R368. It is seen in 1953 in
Academy Street, Inverness, still in
Alexanders blue.

The early Highland fleet was a really mixed bunch, and included
A110, a six-wheel 1937 Albion SPPW145 with Cowieson
39-seat body. It had been new to Young, Paisley, and passed to
Highland with the Macrae & Dick fleet. It is seen in Inverness in
1953 and *inset* is a similar vehicle in Young colours.

A Highland Transport vehicle which did not last into the Highland Omnibuses fleet was this 1930 AEC Regent with 50-seat Strachan body. It was originally an AEC demonstrator, and passed to HTC in 1931.

The early Highland fleet included several utility Bedford OWBs with Duple or SMT bodies, and one is seen at John o'Groats in 1953.

There was a long tradition of Guys in Highland, dating back to HTC days, and the fleet was augmented in the 1950s and 1960s with single-deckers and double-deckers transferred from other SBG companies. K22 had a uniquely-styled version of the Alexander Coronation body on Guy Arab UF chassis, and was exhibited at the 1952 Commercial Motor Show. It was new to Western SMT, and passed to Highland in 1965; it is seen at Farraline Park, Inverness in 1966 in the maroon and cream livery of the time.

MacBrayne services on the island of Harris passed to Highland in 1971, and CD66, a Bedford VAS1 with Willowbrook 28-seat body, is seen approaching Tarbert, Harris, in 1974, in the later Highland poppy red and peacock blue livery. The bus was new to MacBrayne as 204 in 1966.

Above: The main double-deck model injected into the Highland fleet from 1966 to 1976 was the Albion Lowlander, all but one from other SBG subsidiaries. AL40 was new in 1965 to Western SMT, an LR7 model with 69-seat Northern Counties body. It is seen on an Inverness town service, Highland's main double-deck requirement, now receiving Daimler Fleetlines.

Below: At Inverness in 1974, two of Highland's lightweight single-deckers. T60 was one of many Willowbrook-bodied Ford R1014s, while CD75 was a Bedford SB5 with Willowbrook 39-seat body, new in 1970, but originally ordered by MacBrayne.

John Sword's large Midland Bus Services fleet was bought by SMT in 1929, and in 1932 was transferred to Scottish Transport — soon to be renamed Western SMT. For a time, some of the Midland buses wore an unusual unpainted aluminium 'livery', like this normal control Albion being prepared for service at Airdrie in 1930.

Caledonian Omnibus Company, of Dumfries, was a Tilling company, and passed to BTC in 1948; following the nationalisation of SMT, the Caledonian business passed to Western SMT in 1950. Among the vehicles acquired were a number of secondhand Leyland Titans, like the two seen here at Dumfries in 1953. 904 was a TD1 Titan new in 1928 to Glasgow Corporation, and passed to Caledonian in 1940. 910 was a TD2 Titan, new in 1932 to Plymouth Corporation, which came north in 1945. The Croft 53-seat body was fitted in 1947.

The Western subsidiary Greenock Motor
Services was operated as a separate
company until 1949. This 1935 Leyland
Lion LT7 had a smart 36-seat Leyland
rear-entrance bus body, but passed to the
main Western SMT fleet in 1946 and
received a new Brush coach body to help
re-start long distance coach services after
the War; a similar rebodied Lion is shown
on page 44.

The smart black and white livery worn by
the Western SMT fleet from the mid-
1930s is still retained for coaches. There
were 29 1935 Leyland Tiger TS7s, with
32-seat Leyland bus bodies, and most
were rebodied as double-deckers during
the war.

A Caledonian bus which did not survive to pass into Western ownership, this was probably 149, a Thornycroft Cygnet with 30-seat Harrington coach body, originally ordered by Harper, Peebles, before that firm was taken over in 1932.

Take-over of Caledonian brought a number of typical Tilling vehicles into Western hands. There were several ECW-bodied Bristols, L5G saloons and K5G and K6B double-deckers. 878 was one of the K5Gs, and was new in 1949; it is seen here at Annan, later in its life.

There were 30 Leyland Lions acquired from various sources in 1946, which received new Brush 30-seat coach bodies to allow Western SMT to resume its coach services after the war. The chassis of VD 3466 was new in 1934 to Central SMT, and is seen in Glasgow preparing to leave on a special hire to Lourdes.

Surprisingly, three of the first Albion Aberdonians were supplied to Western SMT; all Western's underfloor-engined single-deckers before — and since — had been on heavyweight chassis, and the lightweight Aberdonians lasted until 1965, when they were transferred to Alexanders (Northern). 1384 with 39-seat Alexander body is seen at Cove, Dunbartonshire, in 1960.

The 23 1960 Western Leyland Titan PD3/3s had Burlingham 67-seat bodies, virtually identical to previous Northern Counties deliveries. 1572 is seen when new at Gourock; it was withdrawn in 1976.

44

Single-deck deliveries in the predominantly double-deck Western fleet in the years 1952-62 were substantial underfloor-engined chassis with Gardner engines — initially Guy Arabs and subsequently Bristol LSs and MWs. This was 1280, a Bristol LS6G with 41-seat Alexander body, seen at Rothesay, Western's outpost on the island of Bute, in the Firth of Clyde.

As in the Alexanders and Central fleets, Albion Lowlanders succeeded Western's lowbridge Leyland Titans and a 1963 Alexander-bodied example is seen on a school contract duty in Kilmarnock in 1977.

Birth of the Blues

In 1975 the Scottish Bus Group decided to adopt a corporate livery for its fleet of London coaches, which at the time wore individual company colours. A blue and white livery was chosen, with prominent Scottish fleetnames, and an Eastern Scottish Bristol REMH6G, with the distinctive Alexander M type body, was chosen as the prototype. A357, new in 1970, lost its yellow and black livery, and is seen in the Eastern Scottish Marine Works (*top*), without the beading bands, to allow a flat fleetname. The second picture (*above*) shows a coachpainter at work on the blue roof, and the third (*above right*) shows paintshop staff unrolling the fleetname — it had been hand-painted on adhesive vinyl — on the coach side. With the name in position, the change is more dramatic (*right*), but the flush sides were abandoned on the subsequent coaches in favour of a raised metal panel.

The saltire-inspired logo is seen (*left*) in position on the prototype coach. The second prototype, A364, set the pattern for the rest of the Group's motorway coaches, and is seen (*centre*) fresh out of the Marine Works paintshops in December 1975. A side-by-side comparison (*foot of page*) demonstrates the success of the new livery compared with the previous yellow and black colours — both are Eastern Scottish Bristol REMHs.

Prior to the introduction of the blue Scottish coaches, the Western Glasgow–London coaches were painted black and white, like 2537, a Volvo B58 with Alexander body, seen at speed on the M6 near Leyland. The eight Volvos supplied in 1975 are the only Volvo single-deckers in the SBG.

An older Western SMT London coach, a Bristol REMH in the corporate livery, is prepared for service at Kilmarnock.

Local Authority fleets

Major changes in the 1970s affected the whole face of local authority transport in Scotland. First, in 1973, Glasgow Corporation Transport disappeared into the new Greater Glasgow PTE, which is responsible to Strathclyde Region for policy and financial control, and operates along the lines of the six PTEs in England. Then in 1975 the Scottish counties were replaced by nine Regions and three Island Authorities, with responsibility for co-ordinating transport. Three of the Regions inherited municipal bus systems, and these assumed the responsibility for overseeing the transport needs of the whole Region. So the Aberdeen, Dundee and Edinburgh Corporation fleets became the Grampian, Tayside and Lothian transport undertakings.

Aberdeen's first electric tramcars ran late in 1899, and the tramway system expanded over the years. Traditional four-wheel cars were bought until the late 1920s, but in 1940 a batch of experimental cars included two bogie English Electric streamliners. Twenty similar cars followed in 1949, the last new trams built for Aberdeen service. The tramway system closed in 1958.

The first Aberdeen Corporation motor bus was bought in 1920 for touring work, and proper bus services commenced the following year. Thornycrofts and Albions were popular in the 1920s, and these were joined in the early 1930s by Crossleys, many with locally-built bodies by Walker. AECs and Daimlers then became standard, and these makes dominated the fleet, mainly in double-deck form, until the arrival of Leyland Tiger Cubs in 1966. These were followed by several batches of single-deckers including AEC Swifts and Leyland Nationals. The double-deck intake since that time has consisted of Daimler Fleetlines and Leyland Atlanteans with Alexander bodies.

With local government reorganisation, Grampian Regional Transport assumed control of Aberdeen Corporation's buses; GRT retained the Aberdeen colours of Lincoln green and cream, but the livery style was altered, and an orange stripe was added.

Dundee Corporation was just a few months behind Aberdeen with its first electric tram, which operated in 1900, and the tramway fleet was built up gradually until 1930, when the last new cars were delivered. The system lasted until 1956.

Dundee also tried trolleybuses, between 1912 and 1914, and bought its first motor buses in 1921. These were Thornycrofts, but Leylands became popular, including some Titan double-deckers. After experiments with different chassis types, Dundee, like Aberdeen, settled on AECs and Daimlers, and the two undertakings pursued a fairly similar vehicle-buying policy for many years. In the 1960s Dundee moved on to 11metre AEC Swift and Daimler Fleetline single-deckers, and in the 1970s high-capacity 10metre double-deckers — initially Fleetlines, but more recently Volvo Ailsas and Bristol VRTs.

Dundee Corporation Transport became part of Tayside Regional Transport in 1975, and the green Dundee livery was replaced by the smart Tayside blue and white scheme.

Edinburgh Corporation did not electrify its tramway network at the turn of the century, unlike Aberdeen, Dundee and Glasgow, and the adjoining burghs of Leith and Musselburgh. The Edinburgh cable system, first opened in 1888, lasted until ECT completed its electrification in 1923. The system grew until the War, and new trams to a restrained design were built right until 1950. The last tram ran in 1956.

The first Edinburgh Corporation bus ran in 1914, but World War 1 intervened and serious bus operation did not start until 1919. Leylands and AECs were favoured from the start and dominated the fleet, apart from small batches of Karriers and Dennises, until the arrival of various types including Morrises and Daimlers in the early 1930s. Daimlers became standard until the War, but a varied collection of new vehicles was bought during and after the War. Leylands became standard from 1952, apart from batches of Guy double-deckers and Seddon single-deckers.

Edinburgh's coach fleet has been an important part of the undertaking since the earliest motor bus days, and new vehicles were of Leyland, Dennis and Morris manufacture before the War; since then, with a few exceptions, new coaches have been Bedfords.

Lothian Region Transport retained the ECT madder and white livery in 1975, with changes restricted to crests and legal lettering.

The Glasgow Corporation tramway system was electrified from 1898, and expanded to become one of the largest, and best known, in the country. After the famous Standard four-wheel cars, built between 1898 and 1924, came the Kilmarnock Bogies in 1927/28, and the streamlined Coronation cars in 1937-41. The Mk II Coronations — the Cunarders — were built in 1948-52, and Glasgow's last new trams were built in 1954. The system closed in 1962.

The first Glasgow Corporation motor buses were bought in 1924, and AECs, Albions and Leylands dominated the fleet until World War 2. After the War, GCT continued to buy from these manufacturers, and also took large batches of Daimlers. Since 1962 the

Leyland Atlantean with Alexander body has been the standard purchase, with variety provided by small batches of Ailsa and Metropolitan double-deckers. Single-deckers have played only a small part in the Glasgow story, but GCT's successor, Greater Glasgow PTE, has started to build up a coach fleet, using new and converted vehicles.

Glasgow also had a sizeable trolleybus system, but this lasted only from 1949 to 1967.

The other Scottish motor bus-operating municipalities only just come within the scope of this book, and few good photos exist to record their existence. Kilmarnock Corporation ran buses from 1924 until the end of 1931, when operation passed to SMT; Perth Corporation buses lasted until Alexander took over the services in 1934.

The tramcars illustrated in this section belonged to the four main Scottish municipal fleets, but these were by no means all of Scotland's electric tramway systems. In the frantic years between 1898 and 1909, no less than 20 urban electric tramways opened in Scotland, but by 1930 only 12 survived, and seven years later, following the closure of the Dunfermline system, only Aberdeen, Dundee, Edinburgh and Glasgow had trams.

Not all of the electric tramways that sprung up at the turn of the century were municipal systems; just over half of them were company-owned ventures, which were often overtaken by the rapid development of the motor bus, and chose to sell out in the 1930s when the prospect of high capital investment on upkeep and replacement hastened the owners to sell out to the SMT group. Other tramway systems were merged with the four main municipal networks following take-overs or boundary reorganisations.

The proponents of light rapid transit argue that tramways in their modern guise could help some of Scotland's urban transport problems, but for the moment the citizens of the four main cities look as if they will be travelling by bus for some time to come, and only Glasgow's revitalised underground railway and suburban train services will represent electric traction.

A 1953 scene in Aberdeen with 1923 Corporation-built car 62 in Union Street, en route for Sea Beach. This car lasted right to the end of Aberdeen's tramways in 1958.

Twenty fine streamlined bogie cars were
added to the Aberdeen fleet in 1949.
They were built by Pickering, Wishaw, as
76-seaters, but were downseated to 74
in 1952. This view (*upper*) shows the
sleek lines of an unidentified car, while
(*below*) 24 is seen working on the
famous Bridges route between Bridge of
Don and Bridge of Dee.

Union Street in 1936, featuring new
AEC Regal 51, with 35-seat Walker body,
in the centre, while 88 — a 1931
Crossley Condor with 52-seat Walker
body — passes by on the other side.

Aberdeen's wartime vehicle intake
consisted of utility Daimlers, like 138,
seen here under threatening skies in the
1950s after its Duple body had been
extensively rebuilt.

Aberdeen's 1949 deliveries were ten AEC Regent IIIs with 56-seat Weymann bodies. Number 16 is seen leaving AEC's Southall factory.

Front-engined AEC and Daimler double-deckers with preselector gearboxes were standard in the Aberdeen fleet in the 1950s, and 216, a Daimler CVG6 with Metro-Cammell 62-seat body, was one of 15 delivered in 1956.

Two Aberdeen coaches numbered 13. *Right* is a 1948 Daimler CVD6 with Walker body, rebuilt as a forward-entrance coach in 1963 for use on the tour of the city and suburbs; the next generation 13, also seen on touring work (*below*), was a 1968 AEC Reliance with Alexander Y type 45-seat bus body. It is seen outside St Machars Cathedral in 1976, by which time Aberdeen's buses had passed into the control of Grampian Regional Transport. In addition to the new Grampian fleetname and crests, GRT added an orange relief band to the ACT Lincoln green and cream livery.

Above: Aberdeen was the only Scottish Corporation fleet to buy Leyland Nationals; 42, seen here in Grampian livery, was one of three early examples bought in 1973. Grampian bought another 20 in 1976, 10.3metre two-door 40-seaters, like their predecessors.
Below: After buying both Atlantean and Fleetline double-deckers, Grampian ordered Atlanteans for 1976 and 1977, AN68 models with 74-seat Alexander bodies. Number 201, a 1977 delivery, is seen in Union Street when new.

Prewar Dundee — a 1938 scene at
Shore Terrace, with 11, a 1937 Daimler
COG5 with 36-seat centre-entrance
Cowieson body from Dundee
Corporation's once-large Daimler fleet.

The Daimler COG6 figured in the four
Scottish municipal bus fleets in the late
1930s. Dundee's included eight of these
elegant Weymann-bodied 51-seaters
delivered in 1939, and one is seen here in
1953.

Dundee Corporation's first electric trams, delivered in 1900, lasted until 1955 — albeit completely rebuilt. Car 6, seen here towards the end of its life, started as a 57-seat open-top Dick Kerr-built car, received a top cover by 1910, and was rebuilt and re-trucked in 1930/31.

Dundee car 36, a 1921 Hurst Nelson car, seen in 1954 with, in the background, 141, a 1953 AEC Regent III with 58-seat Alexander body.

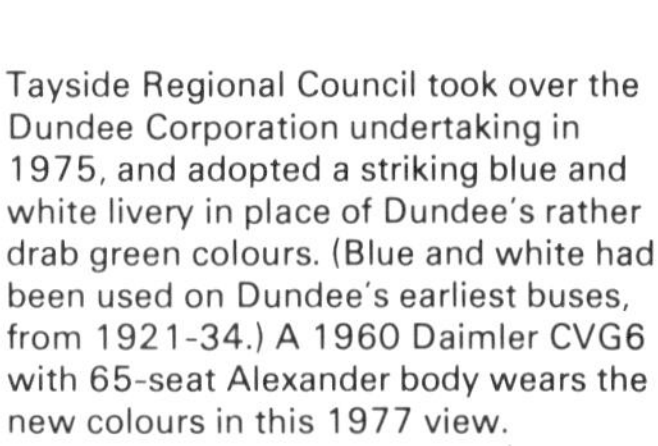

Shore Terrace in 1952, with 1943 Daimler CWA6 utility 150, fitted with a Massey 56-seat body.

Tayside Regional Council took over the Dundee Corporation undertaking in 1975, and adopted a striking blue and white livery in place of Dundee's rather drab green colours. (Blue and white had been used on Dundee's earliest buses, from 1921-34.) A 1960 Daimler CVG6 with 65-seat Alexander body wears the new colours in this 1977 view.

Dundee's ten AEC Reliances with
Alexander 53-seat bodies, had an
unhappy start to life. They were ordered
in 1961, bodied in 1964, but were not
actually able to enter service until 1966.
Number 32 is seen in 1976 in Tayside
livery.

After its AEC Reliances, Dundee turned
to AEC Swift and Daimler Fleetline
single-deckers, before standardising on
high-capacity 10metre Alexander-bodied
double-deckers. The first batch, 83-seat
Fleetlines, were delivered in 1973, and
161 is seen when new in the uninspired
dark and light green livery of the time.

Tayside Regional Council has pursued a rather different vehicle policy from other Scottish local authority fleets. This was the first of many front-engined Volvo Ailsas bought from 1976 onwards. Alexander 75-seat two-door bodywork is fitted.

The Bristol VRT3s delivered in 1977 were frontally similar to the Ailsas, but the engines were mounted at the rear. Tayside 210, with Leyland 501 engine, has an Alexander 83-seat body.

Preservation in Scotland

Bus preservationists are now as active in Scotland as elsewhere in Britain. The very first organised attempt to preserve a bus in Scotland was in 1960, when a group of local enthusiasts bought LJ 2941, a Leyland Titan TD1 with Leyland 51-seat body, which had been in daily use as staff transport for a Johnstone contractor. The bus was new in 1930 to Hants & Dorset; the preservation project fell through and the bus was scrapped.

The Albion Vehicle Preservation Trust is a well-known name in Scottish preservation, and their most familiar vehicle is this Albion Valiant CX39N with Duple 33-seat body, new in 1950 to Hutchison, Overtown, and preserved by AVPT in the colours of Highland, Glenboig.

The Jasper Pettie Consortium is a group of active Scottish preservationists, with a fleet of interesting vehicles. This is ESG 652, preserved by JPC as Edinburgh Corporation 739. It was new in 1948, a Guy Arab III with Metro-Cammell 35-seat rear-entrance body.

Before and after. VD 3433 was one of 110 Leyland Lion LT5As delivered to Central SMT in 1934. It passed to Alexanders in 1945, and received a new 36-seat Alexander body. In 1959 it passed to a Stirling showman, and is seen (*right*) in this role at the Kirkcaldy Links Market in 1960. VD 3433 was bought by JPC in 1973, and is seen (*below*) in its immaculately preserved state, restored to Alexanders livery and painted in Perth town service red. It is shown manoeuvring at the 1977 Dunbar Rally, Scotland's premier bus preservation event.

Another JPC Guy, AWG 393, preserved as Alexanders RO607. It is a Guy Arab III with rare Craven 56-seat body, new in 1948. There were 25 of these buses, and they spent all their lives in the Fife area; RO607 was withdrawn in 1970, and is seen here in 1975 after repainting in its original blue livery.

Another preserved Guy from the Alexanders Fife area — G78, a 1948 Arab III with 35-seat Guy body. It is owned by The Growlers, a preservation group based in Central Scotland.

More typical of postwar Alexanders deliveries, PA171, a 1950 Leyland Tiger PS1 with Alexander 35-seat body, now owned by the Bluebird Bus Preservation Group from Aberdeen.

Two of a kind

There were only two of these Albion KP71NWs ever built — Albion's attempt to build an underfloor-engined model to compete with the chassis from other builders. The model was introduced in 1952, fitted with an 8-cylinder horizontally-opposed Albion engine, 5-speed gearbox and air brakes, but only these two were built. One (*right*) was delivered to Glasgow Corporation, fitted with a 39-seat Scottish Aviation two-door body; it only lasted with GCT until 1959. The second KP71NW also received a Scottish Aviation body, but was a 30-seat coach (*below*). It was loaned to Western SMT from 1952 but was returned to Albion in 1955. It eventually became a caravan, but was rescued for preservation .

The seemingly endless line of stately madder and white trams in Princes Street was for many years a notable feature of Edinburgh life. This early postwar scene features Edinburgh Corporation cars of three different types. Car 156, built in ECT's Shrubhill Works in 1931, incorporated the 1922 Hurst Nelson upper deck previously used to convert an open-top cable car. Car 230, in the centre was one of the first 1934-design Shrubhill standards; it was built in 1935. Car 224 started life in 1903 as a Dick-Kerr-built open-top cable car, and received a McHardy & Elliot top cover in 1923 when the large ECT cable system was converted to electric traction. It was one of the last ex-cable cars to remain in service, and was withdrawn in 1947.

Two more of Edinburgh's wood standards at Haymarket Station in 1953; both were built by ECT in the early 1930s, incorporating older top decks.

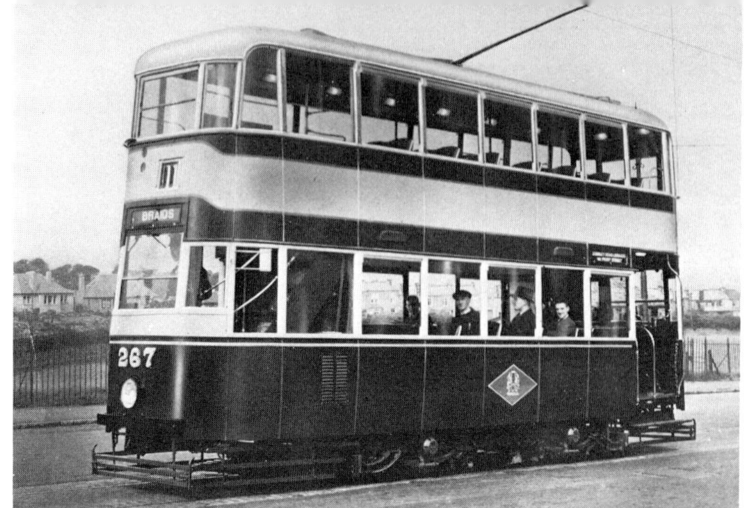

Edinburgh built and bought several experimental trams in the 1930s, including 23 of these 'streamlined' cars from English Electric, Hurst Nelson and Metro-Cammell. Car 267, seen here when new at Braids terminus, was one of three 1934 English Electric trams.

The 84 Shrubhill standards built from 1934 to 1950 dominated the later Edinburgh fleet, sedate 62-seaters like 160 and 223 here, built in 1935 and 1939 respectively. They are seen in St Andrew Square, with Edinburgh's new bus station taking shape on their left.

Last journey for an Edinburgh wood standard in 1954, on board Connell's transporter en route for the Coatbridge scrapyard. Many of Edinburgh's trams ended their lives in this way; sadly, only one Edinburgh tram survived to be preserved — 1948 standard car 35.

End of the road for two of the 300 Metro-Cammell bodied Leyland Titan PD2/20s bought by ECT in 1954-57 to replace the tram fleet. These 1954 examples are seen in 1976 in a Coventry scrapyard.

Above: Edinburgh's standard single-deck model in the late 1930s was the Daimler COG5 with Weymann 36-seat rear-entrance bodywork. Many were extensively rebuilt after the war, including 628, a 1936 bus rebuilt by ECT in 1949, and seen turning in the High Street in 1954.

Right: A rare view of two of Edinburgh's wartime vehicles, photographed near ECT's Central Garage. They are A10, a 1937 Daimler COG5 with Cowieson body, and G63, a 1943 Daimler CWG5 with Massey body, both in an attractive lined-out grey livery. A10 was new with Dundee Corporation with a 36-seat centre-entrance body — similar to YJ 4104 shown on page 56. It was requisitioned by the Ministry of Defence in 1940 for War Department work, but unlike most of its brothers, which returned to Dundee service in 1942, it passed to Edinburgh Corporation along with an older Dundee COG5, and they were extensively rebuilt to rear-entrance 36-seaters, and re-registered. G63 was rebodied in 1954 — see page 70.

After many years of Daimlers, a new transport manager brought Leylands back to the Edinburgh fleet. Among the first deliveries, in 1952, were 16 all-Leyland Royal Tigers with 40-seat standee rear-entrance bodies. 807 is seen when new in George Street; with its brothers, 807 later became a front-entrance coach.

When Edinburgh's older single-deck fleet came up for replacement, Leyland Tiger Cubs with Weymann bodies were chosen, and between 1959 and 1961 100 of these buses were delivered. 15, new in 1959, is seen at East Brighton Crescent, Portobello, used as a turning loop for the 40 and 45 services — though not before protests from local residents had produced a 10mph speed limit, hence the notice on the left.

In the 1950s, Edinburgh had new 8ft
wide bodies fitted on utility chassis, and
the resultant buses proved to be useful
fleet additions. Sixty were ex-London
Transport Guy Arab chassis which were
reconditioned and fitted with new Duple
55-seat bodies in 1952/53. This (*right*)
was 355, in its original ECT form in
Princes Street; like the rebodied
Daimlers, the London Guys received
Leyland-style glassfibre fronts, and all
had been withdrawn by 1969, having
survived longer in Edinburgh than with
London. Although relegated to lighter
duties later in their lives, they performed
sterling front-line work during the tram-
bus changeover, and one is now
preserved. Sixteen of Edinburgh's own
wartime Daimlers received new
Alexander 58-seat bodies in 1954. This
was 63 (*below*) the bus shown in its
original form on page 68; it was a CWG5
model when new, but most of the batch
were originally CWA6s, and only received
Gardner 5LW engines in 1954.
Facing page: Edinburgh City Transport
held its first, highly successful, Open Day
in 1972, and one of the attractions was
1969 Leyland Atlantean/Alexander 342
on the tilt apparatus at Shrubhill Works.
The bus was one of the first ECT batch of
two-door Atlanteans, and the 'dots' either
side of the destination indicators show
that it is a one-man bus.

PAY
ON
ENTRY
Blackhall West End
Melville Dr Newington
Liberton Kaimes
7
KAIMES
PAY
ON
ENTRY
LEYLAND

Framed in the rear window of one of ECT's Birmingham-style Daimlers as it climbs to Clermiston — 845, a 1966 Leyland Titan PD3A/2 Titan with 70-seat Alexander body, one of 25 bought to replace Tiger Cubs on the busy 1 Circle. These were to be ECT's last front-engined double-deckers.

Night-time in Princes Street, with an Alexander-bodied Leyland AN68 Atlantean. This combination became ECT's standard in 1972, and 22 was one of the first batch. The arrow symbols on the front panels indicate that the bus is fitted with the Autofare ticket system.

Scottish local government reorganisation brought little change to the ECT fleet in May 1975. Lothian Region Transport retained the madder and white livery, and simply replaced ECT crests and legal lettering. This was 738, a late survivor of the 300 tram-replacement Metro-Cammell bodied Leyland Titan PD2/20s, and it is shown in 1976, its last year in service, on a short bus-only stretch set up as part of a traffic management scheme at Prestonfield.

The Leyland Atlantean has served Edinburgh well, but there were occasional problems — like this engine fire which temporarily immobilised 285 in 1974. Fortunately, the fire, which was contained in the engine compartment, started as 285 drew into Hyvots Bank terminus; unfortunately, the Scottish Columnist of *Buses* magazine and the Editor of this book were on board with their cameras ...

A rare photograph of a rare bus, a Glasgow Corporation Vulcan Emperor with 48-seat Cowieson body, one of 25 bought in 1931. 353 is seen at Kelvindale terminus. By 1936 many of these buses had been fitted with Leyland engines and radiators.

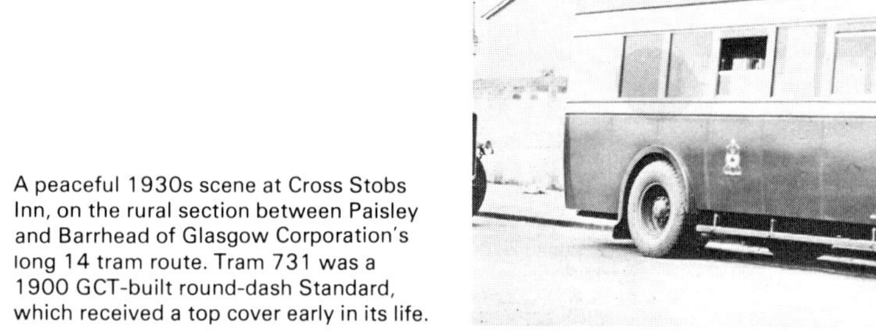

A peaceful 1930s scene at Cross Stobs Inn, on the rural section between Paisley and Barrhead of Glasgow Corporation's long 14 tram route. Tram 731 was a 1900 GCT-built round-dash Standard, which received a top cover early in its life.

The Glasgow tramway network was rightly regarded as one of the great systems of all time, and the Glasgow Standard car was justly famous. 122 was a 1919 GCT-built hex-dash car, photographed in 1956 at Parkhead depot. Parkhead housed trams and buses and Parkhead *Garage* on the bus on the right was the same place as Parkhead *Depot* on car 122. The bus was B26, a 1948 Albion Venturer CX19 with 56-seat Metro-Cammell body.

Glasgow's first double-deck bogie cars were the 51 Kilmarnock Bogies, delivered in 1927/28. Cars 1100 and 1110, shown here at Dalmuir West, were identical when new, but 1100 was rebuilt with streamlined ends in 1941, and also received Coronation-type EMB remote-control equipment. 1100 is preserved at Crich Tramway Museum, Derbyshire, along with standard Kilmarnock Bogie 1115.

While Aberdeen and Edinburgh Corporations bought secondhand trams from Manchester, Glasgow looked to Liverpool for its 46 'Green Goddess' cars — streamlined bogie cars built by Liverpool Corporation in 1936/37, and bought by Glasgow in 1953-55. 1015 (ex-Liverpool 940) is seen here shortly after its arrival in Glasgow. Each car was tested on the route to Cross Stobs, and 1015 is seen in Barrhead on the notorious hairpin bend from Main Street into Cross Arthurlie Street.

The Glasgow tramway tracks were to a gauge (4ft 7¾in) which allowed trams to run on their tyres and railway vehicles to run on their flanges, which are deeper than those of a tram. This meant that it was possible to witness scenes like this in Govan Road until November 1958; here an Andrew Barclay 0-4-0 saddle tank locomotive shunts a truck from Shieldhall goods yard to Alexander Stephen's Linthouse shipyard, past Standard car 83, bound for Shieldhall.

Above left: Glasgow's first new postwar car was 1005, built in 1947 as a single-ended unidirectional car, with entrance and exit on the nearside. In place of GCT's normal green, cream and orange colours, 1005 wore three shades of blue. It is shown here in Hope Street after 1953 when it was repainted in the standard livery, but in 1956 it was converted to become a normal double-ended car, resembling the 'Cunarder' cars which followed it in 1948-52. Its distinctive square tail is seen (*above*) at Maryhill.

Glasgow Corporation scrapped 450 tramcars at its Elderslie Depot, and this 1952 photograph shows a Standard car being pulled over by winch prior to burning.

The late closure of the Glasgow tramway system, in 1962, has meant that several trams are now preserved. One of these is 22, restored as an open balcony car as built in 1922, now running again at Crich Tramway Museum.

The Glasgow Coronation Mk I cars, built mainly between 1937 and 1941, were regarded by many as the finest short-stage passenger vehicles in Europe. They were smooth, handsome and efficient cars, and 1173, seen here, is one of four preserved examples. It is in Glasgow's excellent Museum of Transport, which uses part of GCT's former car works at Coplawhill — the place where most of Glasgow's trams were built. The Museum centrepiece is, fittingly, a fine display of Glasgow trams.

The only prewar RT-type AEC Regent III
built for an operator outside London
Transport was Glasgow 723 of 1940,
with Weymann 56-seat body. It is here in
St Enoch Square in 1956.

Glasgow has never had a large single-
deck bus fleet, and the first postwar
deliveries in 1948 were 43
Daimler CVD6s with ornately-styled GCT
two-door bodies, built on Metal Sections
frames. DS16 is seen on the Clydebank-
Duntocher service in 1950; the apparent
size of the queue suggests that larger
vehicles were required !

The last Daimler single-decker for
Glasgow was DS44, a 1953 Freeline
D650H with 32-seat centre-entrance
Alexander Coronation-style body, which
lasted until 1962.

AECs, Albions and Daimlers dominated
the GCT fleet in the postwar period,
before the Leyland domination started.
A94 was one of 75 1949 AEC Regent
IIIs with Metro-Cammell 56-seat bodies.

D66 was unique in the Glasgow fleet, a
Daimler CVD6 with Mann Egerton
56-seat body — seen here in London on
its way to the 1950 Commercial Motor
Show.

Unpainted buses were tried by several undertakings in the 1950s. Glasgow had one, D95, a 1955 Daimler CVG6, with Weymann 60-seat body, which only remained in this form until 1957. The tin front and bonnet top were painted in the normal orange.

Glasgow's was the last new trolleybus system opened in Britain — as late as 1949. It had a short life — until 1967 — and 34 of these London-style BUT 9641Ts with Metro-Cammell 70-seat bodies were bought to open the system. TB30, seen here approaching Victoria Bridge in 1961, was withdrawn in 1964.

Glasgow built up an unusually large fleet of forward-entrance 30ft long double-deckers in 1960/61. There were 140 Leyland Titan PD3/2s and 89 AEC Regent Vs, like A346 (*above*), with Alexander 72-seat body. Between 1964 and 1969, GCT bought 16 Leyland Panthers with Alexander two-door bodies. LS31, new in 1964, is seen here (*right*) at Pollockshaws shortly after entering service. Glasgow Corporation's bus services passed to the new Greater Glasgow PTE in 1973, and one of the first external signs was the new PTE livery of green, yellow and white.

This 1974 scene shows two Alexander-bodied Leyland Atlantean AN68s, LA804 in GGPTE livery, and LA693 in GCT colours (though with GG logo).

Whoops! When this Leyland Titan PD2/24 from the Glasgow training fleet was deroofed in 1975 (*left*), the opportunity was taken to convert it to a smart open-top vehicle. The job was completed by PTE apprentices, and is seen (*below left*) at Bellahouston Park. It was new in 1958 with Alexander-design GCT Coplawhill-built body.

In 1974/75, Glasgow PTE, with a fleet of around 800 Atlanteans, bought two experimental batches of double-deckers. There were 40 Scania-engined Metropolitans and 18 Volvo Ailsas like AV3, seen here at the semi-rural Carmunnock terminus. These Scottish-built, front-engined Ailsas have bodies by Alexander.

Seventeen years and 1,000 buses separate these two vehicles. LA1 was Glasgow's first Leyland Atlantean — and in fact was one of the first production examples in service in Britain. It is seen in its last active role as a driver training vehicle, in final GCT livery but with 'GG' logo. It is now preserved. LA1000 was exhibited at the 1975 Scottish Motor Show, and represents the standard GGPTE bus, with one-door Alexander body, featuring Edinburgh-style panoramic windows.

The Leopard that changed its spots

Edinburgh Corporation 101 attracted a great deal of attention when it first appeared in 1961. It was a Leyland Leopard PSU3/2R with Alexander three-door body. The rear double doors (*top left*) led to a wide platform, and passengers paid a seated conductor. Exit was by the front or centre doors. It entered service on a double-deck route in 1962 with seats for 33 and standing space for 30 passengers, but was not entirely successful, so in 1963 it re-entered service, with a reduced standee capacity, on the single-deck 1 service (*left*). In 1969, 101 appeared as a front entrance 45-seat black and white airport coach (*below left*), and lasted in this form until 1975, when it was repainted in ECT's normal madder and white livery, fitted for Autofare, and placed in normal service (*bottom left*).

Under the Bridge

The Forth railway bridge has been a popular tourist attraction ever since it was opened in 1890. It has also attracted many photographers, for it is an impressive backdrop. These photos all include the Forth Bridge — or at least part of it. A sunny prewar day at South Queensferry (*top right*), with a 1939 SMT Leyland Tiger TS8/Alexander 35-seater unloading under the bridge piers. A later SOL vehicle at the bridge (*centre right*) — a 1959 AEC Reliance with attractive 38-seat Alexander 'two-day London' body pauses at South Queensferry during the Omnibus Society Presidential Weekend in 1961. On a grey winter day in 1966, SOL BB74, a 1949 AEC Regent III with Duple 53-seat body, sits on the quay at South Queensferry (*below*), ready to depart on the service to Broxburn. By this time, the Forth Road Bridge had been opened, and the ferry service which left from this point had been discontinued.

Stranger on the shore — an unusual visitor to South Queensferry, a Paris Renault TN6 of 1932/33 vintage manoeuvring off the ferry *Mary Queen of Scots* in 1960 with a party of French students.

At the northern end of the bridge, two Alexanders (Fife) buses at North Queensferry on a Sunday School picnic hire in 1964. They are FRO503, a 1945 Guy Arab with utility Northern Counties body, and FPB16, a 1951 Leyland Tiger OPS2/1 with Alexander 35-seat body.

A long way from Twickenham, London Transport RT2565, one of its vast fleet of Park Royal-bodied RT-type AEC Regents, poses at South Queensferry when new, during an international transport conference.

Londoners in Exile

Former London Transport buses have always been popular with Scottish busmen, attracted by London's early retirement and high maintenance standards. Since World War 2 many ex-LT buses have found their way north of the Border, including representatives of the STL, STD, G, RT, RTL, RF, GS and MB families. And not all have been bought by independent operators, for they have also entered service with municipal and Bus Group fleets. The former London G-class Guys appeared in several fleets. This was Alexanders RO703 (London G296), seen (*top*) in Kirkcaldy town service red; it was a 1945 Guy Arab with Northern Counties 56-seat body and when photographed in 1960 at Kirkcaldy Esplanade was still in virtually original condition. SMT also bought ex-LT utility Guy Arabs, though they only ran for a short time in original condition, like Park Royal-bodied GYL 350 (SOL E27, ex-London G211) at St Andrew Square, Edinburgh, in 1952; nine of these were bought that year and were quickly converted by SOL into 30ft long single-deckers for the SOL and Highland fleets. The Craven-bodied RTs found ready homes in Scottish independent fleets, and with Dundee Corporation This was formerly London RT1409, which passed to Garelochhead Coach Services as seen here (*below*).

Laurie (Chieftain), Hamilton, had several ex-London RTL-type Leyland PD2s, and 16 passed with the Laurie business into the Central SMT fleet in 1961. Laurie 47, ex-RTL1464, is seen fresh out of the paintshops in 1959, with RTL1403, still in LT livery, in the background.

Believed to be the first double-decker in the Outer Hebrides — ex-London Country RT3125 leaves the Caledonian MacBrayne car ferry *Hebrides* at Tarbert, Harris in 1976 on a youth club trip to Stornoway.

A rarity in Scotland, and particularly unexpected on the island of Barra, an ex-London Guy Special with ECW body (ex-GS50) in service with McIntyre of Castlebay, Barra, in 1972.

This front-engined Dodge S306 demonstrator visited Hutchison, Overtown, in 1963, though Hutchison, in common with most operators, never bought any. It had a Weymann 42-seat body.

On Loan

Above: A demonstrator which spent lengthy periods with Glasgow and Edinburgh Corporations was 747 EUS, a prototype Albion Lowlander with Alexander 72-seat body; neither undertaking bought Lowlanders. It wore Glasgow colours while with GCT, and a scheme similar to ECT's while in Edinburgh. It is seen in York Place, Edinburgh, in 1963. *Above right:* A demonstration which led to large orders was the visit of 995 EHW to Scottish Omnibuses at Edinburgh early in 1960. It was a Bristol Omnibus Bristol Lodekka FLF6G with 70-seat ECW body, and the Scottish Group took many FLFs.

An advanced model which never really caught on was the Guy Wulfrunian, with front-mounted Gardner 6LX engine, disc brakes and air suspension. The yellow-painted demonstrator 7800 DA visited many fleets, including Scottish Omnibuses — here in Edinburgh in 1960 — but few orders resulted.

Scottish Omnibuses tried German-built Magirus-Deutz and Mercedes-Benz coaches on its Edinburgh-London services in the 1960s. This was OLH 302E, the Mercedes-Benz 0302 demonstrator, outside the National Gallery of Scotland, in Edinburgh, in 1967.

Another overseas representative was this Volvo B59 demonstrator, here working for Glasgow Corporation in 1973. The sophisticated B59 was never accepted in Britain, even, as here, with a Cambridge-built Marshall Camair body. This bus was, in fact, the only B59 to operate in Britain.

Another unique demonstrator was the 37-seat Scania CR145 coach which operated with National Travel and, as shown here, with Scottish Omnibuses in 1974 on the Edinburgh-London express service. The 12metre coach had a rear-mounted Scania V8 engine.

A number of AEC demonstrators found their way to Scotland in the 1950s and 1960s. This was 80 WMH, an AEC/Park Royal Bridgemaster 76-seater, on loan to Scottish Omnibuses in 1959 in the rain at Easterhouse, Glasgow.

The Bridgemaster's successor, the AEC Renown, again with Park Royal body was one of three demonstrators tried by Edinburgh Corporation in 1965. There was 7552 MX, seen here at Waterloo Place, and a Daimler Fleetline and a Leyland Atlantean.

Towards the end of ECT's existence, in March 1975, the Leyland National 10.3metre City Super Bus 35-seat demonstrator visited Edinburgh and ran on service 25 from Turnhouse to Charlotte Square, where it is shown.

EWG 240

An early Leyland Tiger Cub, chassis 520003, was a demonstrator for the Scottish Omnibuses Group, and wore various liveries in its varied career. It started in 1953 in this green and cream livery (*top*), with its stylish Alexander 45-seat body, a design that was to remain unique. In 1955 it was working for Alexanders from Falkirk, where it is seen (*above left*) in cream and blue livery on a local service. When it passed into the fleet of Stark, Dunbar, probably because of its association with Scottish Omnibuses, it was repainted in two shades of green. It is seen as Stark L14 (*left*) at North Berwick in 1959. By 1964, when Stark was taken over by SOL, EWG 240 was in the smart light green and cream livery it wears here (*below left*) at St Andrew Square bus station, Edinburgh.

Edinburgh Corporation's City Tours fleet adopted a black and white livery in 1955, and these pages illustrate some of the coaches which have worn it. The 16 all-Leyland Royal Tiger buses converted to front-entrance coaches in 1958-60 were first painted in this black and white style (*above left*), but were later repainted with less black. The solitary Alexander-bodied Albion Aberdonian, 822, was originally a bus, but soon became a coach (*above*). Another unique ECT coach was 801, a 1951 Alexander-bodied Leyland Royal Tiger (*left*) — again it was formerly a bus. Its contemporary, 802, was a Leyland/MCW Olympic bus which also later became a coach (*below left*). New coaches were bought from 1963 onwards, Duple-bodied Bedfords like 221, a 1964 SB 41-seater (*below right*), seen here at the Palace of Holyroodhouse.

Above left: ECT's Bedford/Duple coaches included several of the six-wheel VAL model; 213 was new in 1964. Unusual additions to the City Tours fleet in 1968 were two Ford R226s, with Duple bodies; 226 (*above right*) is seen in Holyrood Park. Duple Dominant bodies, on Bedford YRT and YMT chassis, were bought for City Tours in 1973 and 1976, and 214 (*right*) is seen in the Canongate. In 1975, ten YRTs with Alexander Y type bodies were bought for tour work, and 114 is seen (*below*) in St Andrew Square in 1975. The following year they were repainted madder and white for bus work.

Independents

As long as the motor bus has been a practical proposition — and even before that — there have been independent operators throughout Scotland. The real pioneers, in the first two decades of this century, opened up many parts of Scotland, rural and urban, in competition with the railways and electric tramways. The buses were basic and often unreliable, and many of the pioneering busmen lacked the sound business sense essential for survival. Some did survive, though, to be joined in the 1920s by a rush of new operators, competing with trains, trams and each other for the business that was there; many used the fast lightweight pneumatic-tyred chassis which flooded the market at the time.

From this chaos came the 1930 Road Traffic Act, and the need to licence crews, vehicles and routes forced many busmen off the road. They were eagerly bought up by the re-formed SMT group, revitalised with railway capital, and many of Scotland's stage carriage and tour-operating companies opted to sell out during the 1930s. The pace of take-overs slowed with the War, and the surviving independents in urban areas were usually survivors from the cut-throat days of the 1920s, who had expanded and consolidated their businesses. Some of these operators sold out to the Scottish Bus Group in the 1950s and 1960s, but there is still a band of staunchly-independent stage carriage operators scattered throughout Scotland.

There is the long-established business of Sutherland Transport, based on Lairg in the remoteness of the Highland Region, providing an essential passenger and mail link between isolated communities. There are other operators scattered along the west coast of Scotland and on the islands, ranging from what are literally one-bus businesses, to larger undertakings like Hebridean Transport, Western Lewis Coaches, Arran Transport and West Coast of Campbeltown. Then there are the larger rural independents, scattered throughout the country from Orkney and Shetland in the north to the Borders and Dumfries and Galloway Regions in the south; and there are the independents in urban areas — particularly the well-known Paisley operators and the Ayrshire co-operatives.

Not strictly independent, but included in this section, are the fast-growing Postbus services; the first service started in East Lothian in 1968 and, since 1972, the Scottish Postal Board has been very active in its development of Postbus services throughout the Scottish mainland and islands, with the 100th Scottish Postbus service starting in 1977.

This section also includes photographs of the once-large bus fleet of David MacBrayne Ltd. The bus business passed with MacBrayne shipping and haulage interests to the Scottish Transport Group in 1969, and the services and vehicles mainly passed to Highland Omnibuses.

The first MacBrayne bus ran in 1906, but this remained a small part of the business until the re-forming of the company with fresh capital in 1928. This allowed expansion of the road services, but until 1941 these were restricted to the mainland, linking Glasgow and Fort William with other parts of the west coast. Acquisition of independent operators brought MacBrayne buses to several of Scotland's islands, but, except for services to Skye, these were abandoned by Highland between 1970 and 1976.

An aspect of Scotland's independent scene in recent years has been the growth of firms offering prestige coaches for hire. Scotland's expansion as a tourist market has created a demand for quality coaches to carry overseas and business travellers to and within the country. The fleets of Dodds of Troon, Doig of Greenock, Little of Annan, Park of Hamilton, Rennie of Dunfermline, Silver Fox of Edinburgh, Southern of Barrhead and World Wide (Scotland) of Lanark have all grown in recent years with expensive new coaches. They, and many of Scotland's stage carriage independents, present a healthy face to the world, with new vehicles and expanding services; they seem determined to maintain their long-standing tradition of staunch independence.

Three of the famous Ayrshire co-operative bus operators survive to this day. AA Motor Services, operating between Ayr and Ardrossan — hence the fleetname — now has just two constituents, Young, Ayr and Dodds, Troon. Over the years AA has operated a wide variety of buses, including this Pickering-bodied Leyland Titan TD7 new in 1942 to Young, Paisley, and seen at Ayr in 1952.

This later AA bus, a 1964 Bedford VAL14 with Willowbrook 54-seat body, appears to be achieving the impossible as it squeezes — just — under the old railway bridge at Barassie in 1967. It was new to Wigmore, Dinnington, and the fleet number, DT No 4, indicates that it was a Dodds contribution.

A1 Service of Ardrossan is still thriving today, with its main route between Kilmarnock and Ardrossan. In 1952 A1 had this ex-Birmingham 1939 MCW-bodied Leyland Titan TD6c, seen here at Ardrossan. It lasted with A1 until 1958.

In recent years, A1 operated an all-double-deck fleet, but before this there were many single-deckers, like BAG 423, one of nine 1946 AEC Regals with Croft bodies. More recently, A1 has started buying single-deckers again.

Two A1 buses laying-over at Kilmarnock in 1955. On the left is GSD 366, a 1956 Daimler CVG6 with Northern Counties 60-seat body — still in active service in 1978 — and on the right is CAG 76, a 1947 Foden PVD6 which had recently received the MCW body from an ex-Liverpool Corporation Guy Arab.

The third, and smallest, remaining Ayrshire co-operative, Clyde Coast of Saltcoats, is represented here by a 1948 ex-Barrow Corporation all-Crossley DD42/4.

One of the better-known independents in Scotland's south west was Murray, Stranraer, which was operating this 1933 Commer Corinthian 24-seater in the early 1950s. The Murray services passed to Western SMT in 1966.

Above right: The smart brown-painted fleet of Carruthers, New Abbey, included this 1950 ex-Ribble Leyland Tiger PS2/5 with Burlingham 35-seat body, seen here at Whitesands, Dumfries. *Right:* A later Carruthers purchase, WGG 623 came from Highland Omnibuses. It was new in 1959 to MacBrayne, a Bedford C5Z1 with Duple Midland 28-seat body, and is seen here in Dumfries.

One of the many smaller tour operators acquired by SMT in the 1930s was James Bowen, of Edinburgh. This 1935 Daimler COG5 with Roberts 32-seat coach body, passed to SMT later the same year, and lasted with SMT until 1945.

Silver Fox is a current Edinburgh independent coach operator, with a modern fleet of smart coaches. This Bedford YRT with Plaxton body, seen at Edinburgh Castle, was new in 1975.

The sole remaining independent stage carriage operator in the Edinburgh area is Wiles, Port Seton, which for many years maintained its main Port Seton-Tranent-Prestonpans service with Albion Nimbuses. This was 330 CTD, a 1957 ex-Leyland demonstrator with 31-seat Alexander body, seen at Cockenzie in 1960.

An unusual vehicle which passed to Ian Glass, Haddington, in 1963 was KSC 738, a Daimler CVD6 with 37-seat Plaxton body. The chassis was new to Robinson, Great Harewood as HTJ 942, and passed to Stanley Mackay, Portobello, in 1953, when the Plaxton body was fitted and the vehicle re-registered.

A more recent delivery to Wiles, Port Seton, a 1975 Ford R1014 with attractive Duple Dominant body. Wiles went to Aberdeen for the registration HSS 1N, as SS was the former East Lothian registration series. It is seen in 1975 on an Omnibus Society Scottish Branch tour.

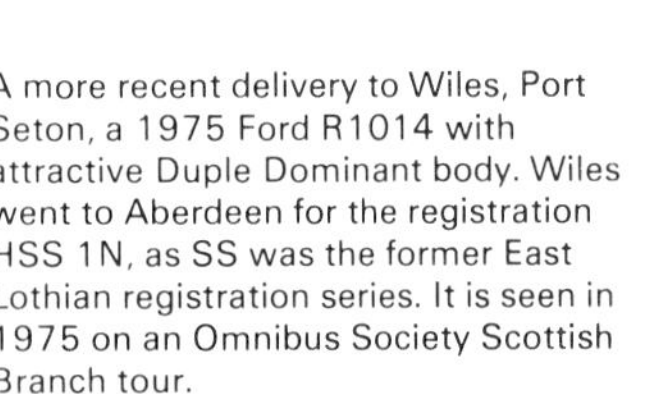

Two Northern Counties-bodied Leylands of Cunningham, Paisley, at Renfrew Ferry, terminus of the service operated jointly from Paisley by Cunningham and Paton, Renfrew. In the foreground is VHE 200, an ex-Yorkshire Traction Titan PD3A/1, while opposite is a 1972 Atlantean PDR1/1.

One of the famous Paisley area independents was SCWS-owned Smith, Barrhead, which was taken over by Western SMT in 1968. In the previous years, Smith had bought four low-height AEC/Park Royal double-deckers, and three of them are seen at the Paisley Abbey terminus. Renown 211 JUS, of 1963, passes 1961 Bridgemasters 30 EGD and 29 EGD.

The smart orange and ivory fleet of
Graham, Paisley, boasted one of
Scotland's first Daimler Fleetlines,
GXS 621 with 78-seat Alexander body,
seen here at Renfrew Ferry shortly after
delivery in 1963.

Like some of the other Paisley
independents, the Graham fleet has
included a larger proportion of single-
deckers in recent years. Here a 1973
Duple-bodied Ford R1014 coach draws
out to pass a 1974 Willowbrook-bodied
Ford R1114, at Paisley.

A well-known bus which was still in the
hands of McGill, Barrhead, in 1978 —
GVD 47, a 1950 Guy Arab III with
Duple 57-seat body, new to Hutchison,
Overtown. It is seen in Paisley in 1967.

Paton, Renfrew, standardised on new single-deckers in the 1970s, but before this the fleet was notable for the constant turnover of secondhand double-deckers — usually Leylands — which passed through its hands. This was FDJ 819, a 1956 Leyland PD2/20 with East Lancs 61-seat body, one of several ex-St Helens Corporation vehicles bought in 1966, which prompted Paton to adopt a St Helens-style scheme for its blue and cream livery.

An older Leyland bought by Paton in 1967 was this ex-Ribble 1947 Titan PD1A with Burlingham body, seen here in the makeshift paint 'bay' at Paton's Renfrew garage.

A wet day at Renfrew Ferry in 1971, with Paton KFS 944, an ex-Edinburgh Corporation all-Leyland PD2/12 Titan 59-seater, new in 1952, and fitted with a Leyland-style front in 1962. It passed to Paton in 1970.

A period scene at Crawford in the 1930s
as GE 6001, a 1929 Leyland Tiger TS1
with Pickering 26-seat body, stops for a
meal break on the road to Glasgow. It
belonged to Lowland Motorways, the
firm which pioneered several long-
distance services between Scotland and
parts of England and which was better
known in postwar days as a stage
carriage operator in suburban Glasgow
until acquired by Scottish Omnibuses at
the beginning of 1958.

At one time, Northern Roadways
competed with the long-established SMT
services from Scotland to London, and
while Burlingham-bodied AECs and
Leylands were favoured, there was also
this 1952 Daimler Freeline with imposing
Duple 30-seat body, complete with toilet
accommodation and buffet. It was first
shown at the 1952 Commercial Motor
Show.

The all-black coaches of Park, Hamilton, have become familiar throughout the country, and purchases in the 1970s have included many Volvo B58s. This 1974 coach, with 12metre Duple Dominant body, was fitted with television, 8-track stereo and other comforts for prestige work like transporting Scotland's top football teams. It is seen with the Rangers team outside Ibrox Stadium, Glasgow.

Cotter, the Glasgow coach operator, always operated a smart fleet. This was JGA 191D, a 1966 AEC Reliance with Duple Commander 47-seat body, seen in Cathedral Street, Glasgow.

One of the first 12metre Plaxton Supreme bodies to be built was fitted to this 1975 Leyland Leopard for Rennie, Dunfermline, whose services include an express facility between Dunfermline and Plymouth.

McConnachie, Campbeltown, was a well-
known operator on the Kintyre peninsula.
This was a Commer Corinthian with
Waveney body, supplied in the early
1930s.

A later McConnachie vehicle, SB 8250
awaits collection at the Duple
coachworks at Hendon, London in 1951.
It was a Leyland Royal Tiger PSU1/11
with rare Duple Roadmaster body, in
even rarer 45-seat *bus* form.

Hutchison, Overtown, operating in industrial Lanarkshire, had two of these AEC Swifts with Alexander W type 53-seat bodies, which were new in 1968. NVD 310F is seen in Wishaw in 1970, the year before it passed, with its brother, to Dundee Corporation.

Irvine, Law, bought this 1960 ex-South Shields Daimler CSG6 with Roe 63-seat body from Tyneside PTE in 1971. It is seen at Law, smartly repainted in City of Oxford-style livery.

The 'other' Irvine — of Salsburgh — operates from its hometown to Airdrie. KGU 34, ex-London Transport RTL584, is seen in Salsburgh Main Street in 1966, still in LT livery.

For some years Scotland boasted two
'Highland' fleets. In addition to the
better-known Inverness-based Highland
Omnibuses, there was Carmichael,
Glenboig's, Highland fleet. This was
HAT 645, a 1947 ex-East Yorkshire
Leyland Tiger PS1 with Weymann body,
which passed to Alexanders (Midland) in
1966 on the take-over of Carmichael.

An earlier Carmichael bus, CVA 105, an
Albion Valkyrie CX13 with Pickering
34-seat body, seen when new in 1946.

On the fringe of the West Highlands lies Garelochhead, and local services are provided by Garelochhead Coach Services. This AEC Regent V with full-front Northern Counties 64-seat body, was new in 1964 and is seen at Helensburgh in 1967.

Recent deliveries to Garelochhead have included Daimler Fleetlines, and Leyland Atlanteans like this 1972 example with Northern Counties body, seen at the company's head office and garage.

The David MacBrayne bus fleet was as much a part of the postwar scene in the Highlands and Islands as was the MacBrayne steamer fleet. The green, cream and red buses were integrated into Scottish Bus Group fleets in 1970-72, following the acquisition of MacBrayne shares by the Scottish Transport Group. At Fort William in 1953 is 80, a 1947 Thornycroft Nippy with Harkness 7-seat mailbus body.

Maudslays were popular in the MacBrayne bus fleet in the late 1940s, and this was 129, a 1948 Marathon III with Glasgow-built Croft 35-seat body.

From 1931 right through to 1970, many
Bedford buses were bought by
MacBrayne. 167 was one of many
Bedford OLAZ coaches with Duple
bodywork bought in 1952. It was a
20-seater with mail compartment, and is
seen at Inverness in 1953 on touring
work.

Three unusual, but attractive, coaches
were bought by MacBrayne in 1952.
They were AEC Regal IIIs with handsome
Roe 35-seat bodies, and 30 is seen near
North Ballachulish in 1963.

A MacBrayne scene at Ardrishaig, with
150, a 1967 AEC Reliance with
Willowbrook 49-seat body, on the
Glasgow service, while 177, a 1958
Bedford C4Z2 with Duple 29-seat body,
is on the service to Oban. Both services
passed to Western SMT.

Six of these AEC Reliances with Duple
Midland bodies were bought by
MacBrayne in 1962, and 390 FGB is
seen at Fort William in 1971 after it had
become Highland B59, although it was
still in MacBrayne livery.

Dunoon Motor Services received SB 5229 in 1937, a 26-seat Albion Victor with Gardner 4LK engine.

A later Dunoon Motor Services purchase, one of several ex-Birmingham City Transport Guy Arab utilities. FOP 356, at Dunoon in 1953, was a 1944 Weymann-bodied example bought in 1949.

Photographed at Dunoon in the hot summer of 1976, SSB 816L of Cowal Motor Services (Baird, Dunoon), a Ford R1014 with Duple Viceroy Express bodywork.

The once-famous line of coaches which used to meet the steamers at Brodick Pier, on the holiday island of Arran. The main vehicles in this 1965 view are a Weir, Machrie Commer Q4/Scottish Aviation; CHH 740, a Ribbeck, Brodick Albion Valkyrie/Duple; SJ 1298, a Ribbeck Commer Avenger/Plaxton; and Lennox DAG 607, an AEC Regal III/Scottish Aviation. At the back is Goat Fell, and the Caledonian Steam Packet car ferry *Glen Sannox*.

Eleven years later at Brodick, and Arran Coaches HCS 350N, a Bedford YRQ with Plaxton 45-seat body, leaves the Pier after collecting passengers from the Caledonian MacBrayne car ferry *Clansman*.

The Arran ferry connects with the mainland at Ardrossan — weather permitting — where Arran Coaches CSJ 400L, a Plaxton-bodied Bedford YRQ, is seen boarding the car ferry *Caledonia*.

The livery attempts to disguise the utility lines of SJ 1024, a 1944 Bedford OWB with Duple 32-seat body, in the fleet of Ribbeck, Brodick. Alongside is SJ 1189, a Commer Commando with Plaxton body.

Another utility Bedford OWB on Arran — SJ 1030 in the Lennox fleet, in 1953. It had a 30-seat Duple body, and was new in 1945.

On the smaller Clyde island of Great Cumbrae, Millport Motors 801 PVK, a Bedford SB1 with Duple body, awaits the car ferry *Coruisk* at Cumbrae Slip.

Waiting at Oban in 1968 before departing on its journey across the Atlantic — the famous Atlantic Bridge at Easdale — Smith, Easdale's, DCU 19, a Bedford SB1/Duple 41-seater.

Winding its way through Skye, from Portree to Broadford, an AEC Reliance/Plaxton in the fleet of Clan Coaches, Kyle of Lochalsh. It was new in 1967 to Essex County Coaches.

An unusual vehicle to find in the north-west of Scotland — 12 EWO, an ex-Red & White Bristol Lodekka FS6B with ECW body, on the Clan Coaches service from Kyle to Plockton.

With more than 100 Postbus services throughout the country, the Scottish Postal Board provides a useful service for otherwise isolated communities. The majority are operated by Commer PB2500 11-seaters like BSF 97L, seen in 1974 at Tigharry, North Uist. *Opposite:* An earlier generation of mail bus, in the fleet of Sutherland Transport & Trading Co Ltd, of Lairg. This rugged-looking prewar Albion, NS 1283, appears to be based on a goods chassis.

This 1960 Bedford C5Z1 with 29-seat Duple body was new to MacBrayne, passed to Highland in 1970, and to MacAulay, Lochboisdale in 1971 with Highland's South Uist services. It is seen at Lochboisdale Pier. *Opposite:* Wick in the 1930s, with a fascinating group of buses, including a Bean and two Chevrolets.

NS1243

EASIEPHIT
SHOES
GREENLEES & SONS
THURSO
MILLED
467
SK1231
SK1468

The bleakness of the island of Lewis is well captured in this view of this 1972 Hebridean Transport Bedford SB5 with Willowbrook 40-seat body, en route from Stornoway to Tarbert, Harris.

The Bedford/Willowbrook combination is very much standard for Lewis. This is Western Lewis LJS 500J, a 1970 Bedford SB5 42-seater at Stornoway Harbour.

MacConnacher, Ballachulish, was a keen
user of small Guy coaches. This was
SB 5348, a 1937 Guy Wolf with Martin
17-seat body.

A later MacConnacher Guy, SB 8155, a
1950 Wolf with 20-seat Ormac body,
which has been preserved.

A varied selection of Bedfords in service in the Shetland Islands. *Above:* A 1958 Bedford SB3 with Plaxton 41-seat body in the fleet of Leask, Lerwick at Toft Voe in 1972. This is one end of the Leask portion of the Overland route from Lerwick to Baltasound on the island of Unst. *Right:* In Lerwick's main shopping thoroughfare, Commercial Street, a Leask Bedford VAM70 with Duple Viceroy 45-seat body passes the Leask office in 1972. *Below:* Photographed in Lerwick, Sandwick Motors VYT 630, a 1959 Bedford SB3 with Duple 41-seat body.

Alexanders (Northern) acquired several independents in Scotland's north-east in the 1960s, including Strachans Deeside Omnibus Service, of Ballater, which was taken over in 1965. This was 25, a 1949 Foden PVSC6, with Roberts 35-seat body, which spent only a short time in the Northern fleet before disposal.

Another Northern acquisition was Simpson, Rosehearty, whose fleet included this 1960 Bedford SB1 with Duple 41-seat body. It is seen near Gardenstown shortly before the take-over in 1966, and it passed first into the Northern fleet and in 1967 was transferred to Highland Omnibuses.

A north-east independent whose services were taken over by Aberdeen Corporation was Rover Bus Service, Aberdeen. Rover 10 was a 1931 Commer NF6 with rear-entrance body, which passed to Aberdeen Corporation with the business in 1935.

A Midland Red-built vehicle was a rarity in a Scottish fleet. Greyhound (T. D. Alexander), Arbroath, bought NHA 580, a 1950 Midland Red S10 44-seater, in 1962 and it is seen in Arbroath.

Two more conventional Greyhound purchases were these ex-Plymouth Corporation Leyland Titan PD2/12s with 56-seat Leyland bodies, seen at Arbroath in 1969.

A rare specimen in the fleet of Smith, Grantown-on-Spey — a 1950 Albion Victor FT39 with Alexander 32-seat body, seen in Newtonmore in 1965. The Smith business was acquired by Highland in 1966.

The well-known fleet of McLennan, Spittalfield, has largely maintained its services with secondhand vehicles. At Spittalfield in 1973 were two vehicles from larger Scottish fleets. GMS 417, a 1955 Guy Arab LUF with Alexander 41-seat body came from Alexanders (Fife), while DRS 364, a 1951 Daimler CVG6 with 1960 Alexander 66-seat body, came from Aberdeen Corporation.

Former Ribble vehicles were very popular with Scottish independents for many years. This 1951 all-Leyland Royal Tiger PSU1/15 coach is seen working for McLennan, Spittalfield, in 1971, by which time it had been converted from centre to front entrance.

Acknowledgements

The photographs used in this book came from many sources, and I am grateful to the contributors who supplied them so readily. The sources, where known, are acknowledged below.

AEC: 13 (2), 52, 53, 82.

Ailsa: 60, 107.

Ian Allan Library: 16, 80, 88, 106, 110, 115, 121, 125.

G. H. F. Atkins: 15, 23.

P. M. Battersby: 28.

Gavin Booth: 8 (2), 9, 13, 14 (2), 15, 16 (2), 17, 20, 21 (2), 22, 23, 28, 29, 30, 35, 40, 44, 46 (4), 47 (3), 59, 61 (3), 63 (2), 71, 72 (2), 73 (2), 85 (4), 86 (2), 87 (2), 88 (2), 89, 90, 91 (3), 92 (2), 93, 94 (5), 95 (4), 101, 102 (3), 103, 104 (3), 105 (3), 107, 109, 111, 118, 126.

Gavin Booth Collection: 9, 17, 18, 33, 38, 41, 44, 66, 79, 86, 93, 101, 108 (2).

A. Brotchie Collection: 106, 121.

Stewart J. Brown: 12 (2), 24, 26 (2), 27 (2), 29 30, 31, 34, 39, 45, 58, 90, 97, 109 (2), 116, 125, 127 (2).

Stewart J. Brown Collection: 18, 19, 37, 43, 126.

W. A. Camwell: 6.

J. A. Cockburn: 31, 55 (2), 60.

G. Coxon: 64, 98, 110, 111, 114.

Duple: 9.

Eastern Coach Works: 36.

Greater Glasgow PTE: 83, 84 (2).

Harry Hay: 44, 90.

D. L. G. Hunter: 10, 68.

R. L. Iles: 93.

Leyland: 32, 35, 42 (2), 107.

I. McKerracher Collection: 20.

Ian Maclean: 12, 43, 51, 64, 75, 76 (2), 77 (3), 79, 81, 82, 92, 93, 99.

Ian Maclean Collection: 74.

Robert F. Mack: 100.

L. Mason: 123.

Alan Millar: 36, 40, 83, 89, 103, 116, 117, 119, 120.

G. R. Mills: 30.

T. W. Moore: 67.

Don Morris: 8, 19, 22, 37 (2), 38, 41, 50, 51, 52, 53, 54, 56, 57 (2), 58, 66, 69, 70 (2), 79, 80, 97, 98 (2), 100, 112 (2), 113, 115, 117 (2).

A. Moyes: 24.

J. E. Openshaw: 34.

A. J. Owen: 56, 65.

John T. Park: 83.

R. B. Parr: 65, 75.

Scottish Tramway Museum Society: 32, 67, 74, 78.

Travel Press: 3, 10, 11, 24, 45, 48, 87, 90.

George F. T. Waugh: 123.

S. N. J. White: 10, 16.

R. L. Wilson: 25, 34, 39, 48, 54, 59, 68, 78, 81, 82, 89, 113, 114, 115, 116, 118, 120, 122 (2), 124 (3), 126, 127.

In addition, I would like to thank Jimmie Blair, Alistair Douglas, Iain MacGregor and Jasper Pettie for their help in providing additional information for captions.